SKITS

THAT TEACH

Teens

Colleen Ison

STANDARD
PUBLISHING

Cincinnati, Ohio

The Standard Publishing Company, Cincinnati,Ohio
A division of Standex International Corporation

00 99 98 97   5 4

Library of Congress Cataloging in Publication Data

Ison, Colleen, 1962-
    Skits that teach teens: including "Three ways to mess up a relationship" and 9 other short dramas / by Colleen Ison.
    p. cm.
    Summary: Includes ten short plays that deal with concerns important to teenagers, including relationships, addictions, prayer, peer pressure, and faith.
    ISBN 0-7847-0108-3
    1. Christian education of teenagers. 2. Drama in Christian education. 3. Christian drama, American. 4. Evangelism plays. 5. Church group work with teenagers. [1. Christian life—Drama. 2. Plays.] I. Title.
BV1485.186   1993
246'.7—dc20   93-304
                                      CIP
                                        AC

Contents

Foreword

Plays are exciting. Being in a play fills people with that mixture of joy, anticipation and terror which tends to bring out the best in them. When people come to a play they come with hope and expectation. They want to be moved to laugh, or cry, or learn something that changes things for them. When Christians weave drama into the life of the church, good things happen.

That's why it's a great idea for youth groups to do plays. Teenagers have all kinds of needs that can be met through drama. In a culture where young people are often viewed negatively, a play gives them a platform to show their talents and get their views across. In a time when so much entertainment is passive and kids are feeling restless and bored, a play gets them fully engaged in working toward a goal.

By performing in even the simplest of skits they learn to overcome fear, to speak confidently in public, and to communicate powerfully.

Best of all, the process of rehearsal and preparation builds unity. Working toward a short-term goal will bring people together faster than anything else. When that goal is a relevant play about Christian life, the benefits are doubled. When the play is then performed for others, the benefits multiply.

The plays in this book are written with the interests and struggles of young people in mind. They are also written with the limitations most youth groups work under in mind, so they are simple, natural, easy to produce and won't cost much.

It is my hope that this book will be a well-used resource in the life of your group.

God bless your theatrical efforts, big and small.

—Colleen Ison

A Word About Words

You can't make the dialogue of teenagers authentic without using a lot of slang. The difficulty in writing scripts for youth groups all over North America is that the slang is different everywhere, and will probably change by next month anyway. This problem has been dealt with in the scripts by following a questionable word with: (or a similar word). Young people can substitute whatever word works best for them. Actually, they can do this anywhere in the script, but they should write down the change and memorize it. Don't allow the cast to think that because they can substitute words they don't have to memorize their lines.

How to Use These Plays

Most of the plays take between five and fifteen minutes to perform. They can be used as a segment of a program, such as an opener for a youth meeting or, with some, as an adjunct to a sermon in a worship service. They could also be combined for a special drama presentation.

One of the plays, "If a Play Could Convert People," is longer and requires full-scale production with costumes, props, scene changes and perhaps lighting. It is approximately half an hour long, so you could flesh out a special program with music and perhaps shorter skits too. Publicity for a special show can also be a youth group task. It provides a good chance to invite family and friends who would not normally attend church.

Another idea is to have a parents' night, where drama is performed by youth but adults are included in follow-up discussion.

Discussion questions follow each script to help when you are using the plays in an educational context. Some of the plays are written in an open-ended way that actually requires follow-up discussion, such as "Three Ways to Mess Up a Relationship" and "The Circle." If you are presenting to a large audience and do not wish to have follow-up discussion, you may still wish to take time to discuss the questions with your cast so they have a deeper understanding of what they are performing.

Tips for Directors

Directing seems like a daunting prospect for some people who are new to the world of theater, but directing a play is much like directing a group in any activity. Here are some things to keep in mind:

—Allow enough time for rehearsal. Too often drama in the church is a poorly-prepared affair. Rehearsal is time-consuming and often tedious, and kids should realize that at the outset. Allow about an hour of rehearsal for every minute of performance.

—Lines should be memorized early on in the rehearsal process. Rehearsal is not for the purpose of learning lines, but for the practice of movement and delivery and work on character. These things cannot really be done with actors who are tied to scripts. Require actors to be off-script early on in the process. After your deadline, forbid scripts on stage. For anyone having memory trouble, appoint a "prompt," to follow rehearsal on a script and supply the needed line, but only when the actor asks for it.

—Suggest that people having trouble learning lines work on them with partners reading all the other characters for them. They could also record the piece on a cassette tape, reading everyone's lines but their own, leaving enough space for them to say their lines with the tape. Remember that cues as well as lines must be memorized. Tell actors you will not have a prompt for the performance. This is a great incentive to memorize.

—A rehearsal tip: Videotape a rehearsal to let actors see themselves. It's worth a thousand director's words.

—Require a commitment from the actors before rehearsals start. Signed contracts stating what is required are helpful. Stress how dependent everyone is on each person to show up on time and not quit halfway through rehearsals.

The contract can specify that latecomers need to apologize to the whole cast, not just the director. You can also add a clause stating that a certain number of late arrivals or no-shows means that person's part is given to someone else. Another suggestion: require kids to audition to get into the cast. This is evidence of high motivation. Resist the temptation to beg kids to be in your play, no matter how good you think they might be. An ounce of commitment is worth a pound of talent.

—Be very affirming. This is so important. People need frequent praise to grow in confidence. Affirmation offsets the tediousness of rehearsal's repetition, and softens your frequent demands that they speak up, slow down, move differently, etc. You will get a great deal more spontaneity and energy from the actors if you praise often and request changes without criticism. You will also have the joy of seeing some of your shy kids blossom.

—Work tirelessly on a few important technical points:

1. Audibility: Do not allow very much rehearsal below required volume. It reinforces the bad habit. Call for louder voices as much as it takes, which will be a lot. Remember that very few people are physically incapable of projecting. They just need to become comfortable with hearing their own voices at high volume.

2. Visibility: Block plays so that actors never need to deliver lines with their backs to the audience. Always correct actors if they do this. Groups need to open out into horseshoes, actors stand on a diagonal that leaves them open to the audience when they are talking to each other, tall people move behind short people, etc. Teach the actors to always be aware of their visibility.

3. Timing: Pay attention to the pace of speech and action. People speed up when they are nervous. Break them of this early on by requiring repetition of lines until they slow down. Another timing problem with new actors is that they take too long to pick up cues, particularly when they are supposed to

interrupt. The skill that overcomes this is listening. If they listen deeply to their cues, their responses will have more natural timing.

—Warm up before rehearsal. Set a positive, disciplined tone from the beginning. Get the actors in a circle and take some time for them each to briefly say how they are doing. Require the rest of the group to listen without talking. This establishes attentiveness and unity. Pray for the rehearsal and the show, including prayers for the audience to have open hearts. Then you can do some warm up exercises that get people moving and work on the three technical areas mentioned. (Many common icebreakers and games serve this purpose.)

A good warm-up time gets people relaxed and working well together. Resist the temptation to be too task-oriented and dive right into practice. Nurturing and building up the kids is just as important as the final product.

—Prohibit put-downs in rehearsal. They are very destructive.

—Be clear about who's directing. To avoid too many chiefs, suggest that anyone with a directing idea suggest it quietly to the director rather than delivering it themselves. This also protects struggling performers from getting too much advice.

—If you have a problem with a kid's behavior, correct him in private. Public discipline is shaming for people.

—Along with tons of praise, set high expectations for the cast. They will usually meet them.

—Most important of all, have fun!

Glossary of Stage Terms

Here is a list of terms used in the stage directions:

Downstage: Toward the front of the stage, toward the audience.

Upstage: Toward the back of the stage, away from the audience.

Stage Right: The actors' right.

Stage Left: The actors' left.

Wings: Areas to the sides of the performing space where actors wait to enter and exit, not visible to the audience.

Line: Each time an actor speaks, regardless of how many lines on the page are filled.

Cue: Whatever comes before an actor's line or move to let him know that it is time for him to do something. i.e. "The cue for your entrance is when she yells 'Help'."

Freeze: Actors suddenly become completely motionless. They can blink but not move their eyes around.

Blocking: The pattern of movement in the play. The director usually has blocking figured out before rehearsal.

Abbreviations

Here is a list of abbreviations used in the scripts, with a diagram showing stage directions:

DS: Downstage

USC (or UC): Upstage center

US: Upstage

DSR (or DR): Downstage right

SÇ (or C): Center stage

DSL (or DL): Downstage left

SR (or R): Stage right

USR (or UR): Upstage right

SL (or L): Stage left

USL (or UL): Upstage Left

DSC (or DC): Downstage center

USR	USC	USL
SR	SC	SL
DSR	DSC	DSL

Audience

If a Play Could Convert People

In this one act play, three goofy skits are framed with dialogue between two church youth group members who are disagreeing about what to do for their annual drama production. George wants to come up with an awesome play that will convert all unbelievers in the audience; Jessica tones down his wild ambitions with common sense and dry humor. The play operates on two levels; amusing the audience with George's ridiculous ideas, at the same time communicating the love of God to unbelievers and a call to Christians to live their faith authentically.

Cast

George—A giddy, idealistic person, also a faithful, zealous Christian. Lots of lines.

Jessica—George's intelligent, realistic, slightly cynical friend. Also lots of lines.

Person 1

Person 2

Person 3—Just one line.

Troubled Person—Does comical mime and sound effects.

Mugger 1—No lines, short mime scene.

Mugger 2—No lines, short mime scene.

Christian 1—No lines, several minutes of mime.

Christian 2—No lines, several minutes of mime.

Unbeliever—Lines and fairly involved mime. A depressed, cynical person.

Believer—Lines and fairly involved mime. A goody-goody.

Israelites—3-10 people who mostly stand still.

Egyptians—3-10 people. A rowdy bunch.

Red Sea Crowd—The more the better, at least 8, can be children. They do a lot of dramatic movement and enthusiastically attack the Egyptians.

God's Voice—A pleasant male voice speaks into a microphone offstage.

Costumes

Jessica, George and everyone in the opening discussion, as well as the Christians in the first skit, wear casual clothes.

The Troubled Person can either wear a business suit and carry a briefcase, or wear some kind of blue collar work clothes and carry a lunchbox.

Punks can wear anything that makes them look mean, dangerous and antisocial.

The Believer and Unbeliever should wear the same thing; some kind of pajamas.

The Israelites can wear choir robes.

The Egyptians can wear bathrobes with cloth headdresses secured with headbands. They carry toy weapons such as bows and arrows and clubs.

The Red Sea Crowd should all wear red costumes, *(or at least red T-shirts)* and carry red scarves or pieces of cloth to wave around. They can tie red scarves to their arms and legs too.

Production Notes

Have a ladder USC and four chairs or blocks on stage at the opening of the play. These are the only things that will be needed throughout the play, and George will set them up as part of his business. The ladder can be used to lean on or climb on during dialogue. The chairs or blocks are used for sitting, lying down, and standing on when different levels are needed.

The Red Sea scene is a good place to use a lot of people who do not have to rehearse much. If you are short of teenagers you can use younger children.

If you have use of lighting, you can distinguish scenes from the dialogue sections with spotlighting. Also spotlight George when God is speaking to him at the end, and instead of having George exit at the end, fade the lights down with him still looking up at God.

During rehearsal, agree on a "God-spot" somewhere on the ceiling so George and Jessica are looking at the same place.

You will need some kind of public-address system with an offstage mike to do God's voice. This can be as simple as a microphone hooked up to a guitar amp. if your building does not have a PA system. If you can not find a recording of "angel" singing, or don't have someone to fade music up and down, you can skip it and just have God's voice saying, "George" be the cue for George and Jessica to look up.

The Script

The scene begins with Jessica, Person 1 and Person 2 on stage. Jessica is leaning on a ladder UC, holding a clipboard and pen, Person 2 is sitting on a block DSR and Person 1 is spinning idly in an office chair SL.

JESSICA: Come on you guys, we've got to be able to come up with something.

PERSON 1: But George always comes up with the ideas, every year. It's a church tradition.

JESSICA: Not this year. If we put on one more play that flops they're not gonna let the youth group do any more drama. I heard Pastor *(or whatever your church's title)* say that to the Youth Minister.

PERSON 2: I wouldn't call all George's plays flops.

JESSICA: OK. How about catastrophes?

PERSON 2: But Jess, he's so into doing this. Drama's his thing.

PERSON 1: Really. If he finds out we're trying to cut him out of this he'll be emotionally destroyed.

JESSICA: Oh, come on. We're not talking about a Broadway production here.

PERSON 1 *(still spinning):* George thinks our church plays are of national significance.

JESSICA *(getting exasperated, she moves over to Person 1 and stops him spinning):* Listen. Don't you remember how you felt after the last play? You were sitting backstage over there *(She points.)* in this very chair, covering your face and all you could say was "This isn't really happening," over and over and you *(Turning toward Person 2.)* ran out into the audience as soon as it was over shouting, "I had nothing to do with this!"

PERSON 2: I was a little upset.

JESSICA: You guys really want to go through something like that again?

PERSON 1: It's hard to stay mad at George. Maybe it wasn't as bad as we're remembering.

JESSICA: Get real. He released 700 pigeons into the sanctuary! It was like the Hitchcock movie. Kids were hysterical, people were stepping on each other to get out. We had to hold eight fund raisers to pay for the damage!

PERSON 2: I forget—why did George do that?

PERSON 1: He wanted doves but he couldn't find that many. He wanted a bunch of doves to go fluttering up to the altar to symbolize the presence of the Holy Spirit.

JESSICA: They did more than flutter up to the altar.

PERSON 2: Right on Miss Livingston's head. George should have thought of that.

JESSICA: I'm glad these little details are coming back to you. Remember the year before?

PERSON 2 *(smiling):* The cherubs? Well, that wasn't a bad idea either. It would have been cute to have cherubs floating down from the choir loft and landing around the sick baby's bed. Too bad the support beam broke.

PERSON 1: Yeah. But you know, it really was a miracle. All those cherubs plunging into the audience and no one was injured. Maybe the wings broke the fall.

Person 2: George said it was a graphic illustration of divine providence.

JESSICA: Come on, you guys, face it. George is one of my best friends, but he can't be trusted with a play. Why anyone let him keep going after his first try is a mystery to me.

PERSON 1: Oh yeah. I had forgotten about that. Moses and the burning bush.

PERSON 2: Well, we were overdue for a new building anyway . . .

(Person 3 enters, breathless.)

PERSON 3: You guys, George found out you're talking about the play. He's coming this way, and he says he's got an idea!

(All look at one another in alarm.)

PERSON 1: Well, Jess, you said he was one of your best buddies.

PERSON 2: Yeah, I guess you're gonna need some privacy.

(They all move to exit except Jessica.)

JESSICA: Thank you guys. Thanks a lot!

(George enters, breathless, excited.)

GEORGE: Jess—hi! You're alone? Oh well. Listen, I heard you started the play. I must have missed the announcement, but don't worry. Man, I have got the most awesome idea!

JESSICA: Uh, George—

GEORGE *(interrupting):* It's great. It's profound. You're gonna be excited. I got inspired at work today. I'm putting extra pepperoni on a medium thin crust, and this thought comes out of nowhere—

JESSICA *(interrupting):* George! Wait. Your ideas have gotten us into some heavy-duty trouble. This play is our last chance to—

GEORGE *(interrupting):* No, no, it's not like that! I've given up the sensational stuff. Jessica *(Becoming serious.)* I'm in a new phase. I have now entered the realm of hard-hitting spiritual truth. I'm not out to wow people anymore. No more Spielberg rivalry. I'm going beyond entertainment—I'm going for conversion!

JESSICA: Conversion?

GEORGE: Yeah. *(Taking her arm and moving her forward.)* Jess, wouldn't it be amazing if we could do a play that would convert people? *(In his excitement, George begins pacing back and forth, and ends his speech by leaping onto the ladder, striking a triumphant pose, and looking expectantly at Jessica.)* Imagine—a moving, sensitive drama leading the masses to faith in Jesus Christ. You could round up all your party animal friends and all your teachers who think Christians are intellectually impaired and all your relatives who think you're going through a phase—and bring them to this marvelous play, where they are overwhelmed by a complete understanding of the truth. I'm gonna come up with a play like that.

JESSICA *(not at all excited):* Tall order. Assuming they come.

GEORGE: Nothing is impossible with God.

JESSICA: So what's this play about?

GEORGE *(descending from his ladder):* Well, I haven't worked on details like plot or characters yet. But I know this much Jess. Everyone has some kind of pain in them, right? And if your play could show people how much God wants to help them and comfort them, they would all become Christians on the spot. So we've got to show them that God can take any life, no matter how messed up it is, and make it into something new.

JESSICA: Uh-huh.

GEORGE: Uh-huh. So, let's come up with a character who's in a lot of trouble. It has to be something that people can identify with. Let's say it's a guy who just lost his job. *(George takes Jessica's arm and moves her to the side of the stage.)* OK, he enters . . .

(Troubled Person enters as George grabs a chair and brings it DC. Troubled Person slumps into the chair and stares blankly.)

GEORGE: He's sitting on a bus, wondering where on earth he'll find another job. Let's say a computer replaced him and his skills are obsolete. Yeah. *(Pauses, thinks.)* Now, I think we need some other kind of rotten thing to happen so more people can identify with him. Let's say, he's sitting there all desperate; his finances, future and self-esteem down the tubes, and a couple of punks get on, mug him and steal his last check.

(Punks enter, mug him, steal his wallet and exit. He is left slumped over in the chair.)

JESSICA *(taken back)* : Oooh.

GEORGE: Yeah. Now he's really in bad shape. But you know, there are a lot of people who still couldn't identify with him. *(Pauses, thinks.)* What he needs is an illness; some sort of chronic illness.

JESSICA: Is that right?

GEORGE: Let's see. It's got to be dramatic enough to provoke compassion, but not so bad that he couldn't work and take the bus . . . I know. Let's give him asthma.

(Troubled person, still slumped, jerks his head up and begins to take huge, rasping breaths. Jessica looks on in alarm.)

GEORGE: Yeah. That's good. Good. So he's lost his job, been mugged and he's suffering from an asthma attack.

JESSICA: Anything else?

(Troubled Person wheezes more quietly so George can be heard.)

GEORGE: Actually yes. There's something we're not covering— His inner life. You know, like mental health. Lots of people seem fine, but they're in all this emotional pain. Let's make him depressed. Lots of people are depressed. Let's say he's plagued with constant performance anxiety resulting from a deprived childhood.

JESSICA: George! How are you gonna show that while he's sitting alone on a bus?

(Troubled Person interrupts his gasping to throw back his head, shouts "OH NO! Only 90 percent on my finals! They'll ground me for the summer!", and slumps back, gasping again.)

JESSICA: George, is this going anywhere?

GEORGE: Sure, I'm just getting to the climax. Because you see, what's going to happen is that two Christians are just going to happen to get on that bus!

(He beams expectantly at her, as though he has made a brilliant final statement.)

JESSICA: Yeah?

GEORGE: Well that's it.

JESSICA: What do you mean "That's it"? What do the Christians do?

GEORGE: Well they help him of course.

(Christians enter, see Troubled Person and rush to him. They continue to mime the actions which George describes in the next paragraph, in fast motion, which obviously makes it rather comical.)

GEORGE: They rush over to him, prop him up, one of them finds his inhaler and helps him use it. *(Troubled Person smiles and sighs with relief.)* They take him off the bus at their stop, and in the next scene they pray for him and his asthma is totally healed. Their concern lifts his depression, *(Christians pat him on the back)* they give him a job in their cosmetic distributorship. *(They quickly lead him a few steps forward, fix his hair, brush off his clothing and shake his hand.)* They take him to church and for the first time he learns that God loves him. *(They line up either side of him and mime singing a hymn while Troubled Person looks up and smiles)* . . . I mean, this whole part goes without saying. *(Actors freeze as Jessica cuts in.)*

JESSICA: Wait a minute George. Think about this. That's a nice story, and I know things like that are always happening, but don't you think that condensing it all like that might make it seem kind of farfetched?

GEORGE: Farfetched?

JESSICA: People aren't gonna believe it unless they see it in real life.

GEORGE: Oh. It never occurred to me that someone wouldn't believe it. So you don't think it lends itself to the stage?

JESSICA: Right. Save it for a movie.

GEORGE: That's OK. I've got another idea. *(To the actors.)* I guess you guys can take off. *(They exit. Then he speaks to Jessica.)* Maybe I am trying to fit in too much. . . . Maybe people would identify better with little everyday situations. You know, that's an idea. We could show how much of a difference having Jesus with you all the time makes in everyday life. How things are different even if life doesn't change. If people could get an idea of that difference, nothing would keep them from God!

JESSICA: How are you gonna do that?

GEORGE: Uh, keep it familiar, mundane. Yeah, we've been too theatrical up to now; with all those angels and togas and heroin addicts. Let's just have two guys getting ready for work.

JESSICA: That'll bring them in.

GEORGE: Well, we're showing a contrast, see. We'll divide the stage down the middle, and have someone who knows about Jesus on one side, and a guy who doesn't on the other side, doing exactly the same things, but with different attitudes. We'll have them speaking their thoughts out loud. Like this . . .

(Believer and Unbeliever enter from opposite sides, and for the whole scene, they match each other's mimed actions, with some variations as mentioned. First, they lie down and snore. An alarm rings offstage. They shut off the alarm. Unbeliever struggles up and lights a cigarette. Believer springs out of bed and stretches with enthusiasm. For the whole scene the Believer is unbelievably cheerful and the Unbeliever is miserable.)

UNBELIEVER: God, it's Monday.

BELIEVER *(smiling sweetly):* God, it's Monday! Thank you Lord for another week; a week of new experiences, challenges and opportunities for ministry!

(They look out a window, each looking offstage on his own side.)

UNBELIEVER: Oh no! It's snowing again.

BELIEVER: Snow! It's like magic to wake up to the world carpeted in white!

UNBELIEVER *(putting down the cigarette):* I'll have to shovel the driveway.

BELIEVER: Why, there's a cardinal sitting on that branch—a splash of red against the pure white snow. What a delight to the spirit.

(They each mime putting on a bathrobe.)

UNBELIEVER: The kids'll come in caked with snow and there'll be little puddles all over the floor.

BELIEVER: I can make a snowman with my students at recess!

(They mime going to a refrigerator and opening the door.)

UNBELIEVER *(brightening a little):* Hey, maybe there's enough snow for school to be cancelled. I could go back to bed.

BELIEVER: I hope school isn't cancelled. There's so much to teach the children in every precious day.

UNBELIEVER *(shutting the refrigerator door in disgust):* I feel sick. How can people face breakfast at this hour. I need a cup of coffee. *(Makes coffee.)*

BELIEVER *(taking out several items of food, and putting them on the counter):* How blessed I am to have enough to eat. Praise the Lord.

UNBELIEVER *(staring off into space):* I need a vacation.

BELIEVER *(staring off into space):* I must mail that check to World Vision . . .

JESSICA *(makes a time-out motion):* Stop! That's enough!

(The actors freeze, still staring into space.)

GEORGE: What? What's the matter? I was just getting started.

JESSICA: I'm sorry. I can't stand anymore.

GEORGE *(surprised):* Why not?

JESSICA: Because George, the Christian was making me sick. I mean, I'm on this guy's side! *(She gestures to the Unbeliever.)*

GEORGE: What do you mean, you're on this guy's side? He's got a hangover on a Monday morning. He's a downer! *(To Unbeliever.)* Go away. *(Actor breaks freeze and exits.)*

JESSICA *(to Believer):* You too! *(Actor breaks freeze and exits.)* George, the Christian was just too good to be true. I sure don't act like that in the morning.

GEORGE: Well you should. You've got reason to.

JESSICA: I know! Don't preach at me. Look, I'm not knocking the concept, but it doesn't come across as realistic.

GEORGE: But it is! I used to feel like that guy *(Points to the Unbeliever's side of the stage.)* and now I feel like that guy. *(Points to the Believer's side of the stage.)*

JESSICA: I believe you. I think that's great. But it's really hard to show an audience, from the outside, what's going on on the inside.

(George sits, dejected.)

GEORGE: Well Jess! If I can't get across the miracles God does because they seem farfetched, and I can't get across the happiness He gives you because it makes people sick, how's anyone gonna get converted?

JESSICA: Maybe you shouldn't try to be so direct about this stuff. People kind of need to discover it for themselves. Maybe the most you can do, with a play, or anything, is give people a glimpse of what God's like.

GEORGE: A glimpse . . . *(Suddenly very excited.)* No, Jess— we're gonna do more than that. We've gotta give them a foundation. Yeah. It just came to me. The reason people don't believe that God could be active in their lives today is that they don't know how much God's done in the past. We've got to bring the mighty acts of God in history back to life!

JESSICA *(under her breath):* Uh-oh.

GEORGE: People don't know their Bibles anymore—we need to do a dramatic version of the Old Testament!

JESSICA: The whole Old Testament, George?

GEORGE: Well, we'll hit the high spots. Like the parting of the Red Sea; God performing a supernatural act to deliver His people from slavery to the Egyptians! That is such an awesome story. If people knew how awesome God was they'd be crawling on broken glass to become Christians!

JESSICA: Hang on a sec. You're not planning to flood the sanctuary with 5,000 gallons of water or anything are you?

GEORGE: Well Jess, we've gotta have a little realism. We've gotta use something wet if a bunch of Egyptians are gonna get drowned.

JESSICA *(threatening):* George! If you damage any more property you're the one who's gonna be drowned!

GEORGE: OK, OK, no damage. We'll be symbolic. Uh, let's see. . . . We'll have people being water. Yeah. That'll work. Their graceful, thrashing movements will illustrate the force of the element that God subdues!

(George clears the central stage area, placing the ladder USL and everything else out of the way. Only the ladder will be used again. As he finishes this, possibly with Jessica's help, the Red Sea Crowd enters and occupies the area. They move slowly, gently waving their scarves chest level and lower.)

GEORGE *(directing the Red Sea):* That's it you guys, you're being waves; not too high yet. *(To a younger cast member.)* Hey, stop chewing on that scarf. *(To Jessica.)* OK, there it is. We've got the Red Sea. I think we should narrate the story out of the King James Version—it's so poetic.

JESSICA *(under her breath):* That's fine, unless you want someone to understand it.

RED SEA MEMBER 1: Can we drown people now?

GEORGE: Not yet.

(George goes into the audience and gets a King James Bible [into which the following verses from Exodus 14 have been pasted in], which has been planted in a pew, excusing himself to the people seated there, and returns to the stage. The Red Sea crowd is losing enthusiasm.)

RED SEA MEMBER 2: How long do we have to be waves?

RED SEA MEMBER 3: I gotta go potty. *(Or, to the bathroom, depending on age.)*

GEORGE: OK you guys, be patient. You can stop for a minute. No breaks yet though. This is serious business. You can't be stopping an epic drama every time someone has to go to the bathroom. All right. Now we need some Israelites to be fleeing from Pharaoh's army of evil Egyptians. They need to be dignified, fearless, noble—the chosen people of God.

(Israelites enter R, looking pompous, moving stiffly. In contrast to the Red Sea crowd, they stand perfectly still without expression , USR.)

GEORGE: OK, excellent. Listen everyone—we're gonna take it up where Pharaoh found out that Moses has led the Israelites out of Egypt and has sent his huge army out to nail them. *(Calls offstage.)* Do we have some Egyptians ready back there?

OFFSTAGE VOICE: Yup. Ready.

GEORGE: Good. Pharaoh thinks his army can trap them by chasing them up against the Red Sea. Boy, are they in for a surprise. . . . OK Jess, are you ready for this?

JESSICA: Probably not.

GEORGE: Trust me. This'll work. *(To all.)* OK, we're ready. Here we go. Red Sea—now!

(Red Sea begins to make waves again, adding a quiet splashing sound effect which will grow in volume as the sea becomes more turbulent. George runs up the ladder with the open Bible, strikes a noble pose and begins to read loudly and dramatically. Jessica moves to the sidelines to watch.)

GEORGE: "And Moses said unto the people, Fear ye not, stand still, and see the salvation of the Lord, which he will show to you today: for the Egyptians, whom ye have seen today, ye shall see them again no more for ever. . . . And Moses stretched out his hand over the sea." *(George stretches out his hand.)*

(The Red Sea crowd moves more, and faster, throwing their scarves into the air to make bigger waves, and splashing more loudly. George tops their volume.)

GEORGE: . . . "And the Lord caused the sea to go back by a strong east wind all that night, and made the sea dry land, and the waters were divided!"

(Red Sea crowd, now moving rather violently, parts in one coordinated move on the word "divided," half to each side of the central area, leaving a tunnel down the middle. As they part, they all yell "Swoosh!!" While they are parted they make a new noise, keeping it loud to maintain the energy. They should make a sound to suggest suspense; a repetitive "Ah, ah, ah," sound, or some well known tune like the theme from the "Exodus" movie. They also stand on tiptoe, waving their scarves over their heads but not into the cleared space.)

GEORGE: . . . "And the Children of Israel went into the midst of the sea upon the dry ground: and the waters were a wall unto them on their right hand, and on their left."

(Israelites file, one at a time, to USC and then down through the cleared area, turn sharply DSC and walk DSL where they face the audience and stand, still stiff and expressionless, until they are all reassembled. Then altogether, they throw a fist in the air and shout "Yes!" then return to standing still.)

GEORGE *(hands still outstretched):* . . . "And the Egyptians pursued and went in after them to the midst of the sea, even all Pharaoh's horses, his chariots, and his horsemen. . . . And the waters returned, and covered the chariots, and the horsemen, and all the host of Pharaoh."

(As he is still speaking, the Egyptians run on USR with weapons, and dash into the clearing, yelling and screaming. On "returned," the Red Sea crowd yells "Swoosh" again, and throw themselves into the clearing. A free-for-all follows, with the Red Sea crowd throwing themselves at the Egyptians, waving their scarves around, tackling them, etc. To avoid injuries, make sure the weapons are dropped before the attack. George, who is still in his noble pose, observes that the Egyptians are not obediently drowning but are engaged in battle and play all over the stage. He leaps off the ladder, breaks character, and commands them to die. At first his tone is reasonable, but as they ignore him he becomes more forceful, going to them one by one and pushing them down and finally shouting a hysterical "Die Now!!" They obey at last, giggling. The Egyptians sprawl out on the ground and the Red Sea crowd lays either themselves or their scarves over them. George shakes his head in disapproval, regains composure, climbs the ladder and gets back in character.)

GEORGE: . . . "Thus the Lord saved Israel that day out of the hand of the Egyptians."

(Israelites turn stiffly to a partner, give one another high-fives and return to standing still. George holds a noble pose. There is a moment of silence. George breaks it by breaking his pose and jumping off the ladder. Jessica slowly rises and joins him SL, surveying the scene. She is trying not to smile.)

GEORGE: So, what do you think? Pretty awesome, huh?

(Against her will, Jessica bursts out laughing.)

GEORGE: What are you laughing about?

JESSICA: George, it's a zoo!

GEORGE: Well, it got a little out of control but we'll work with that.

JESSICA *(stepping over a few Egyptians):* It's a great comedy George. *(Walking over to the still-frozen Israelites.)* Especially these guys. They're so—comatose.

GEORGE *(irritated):* They're not comatose. They're dignified.

JESSICA: Don't get mad George. You might not have meant it to be a comedy, but it is a comedy. Couldn't you just, go with it?

GEORGE *(despondent):* I don't want a comedy! I want an awe-inspiring demonstration of the power of God! I want to blow people away!

EGYPTIAN: Hey George. This hurts. How long do I have to be dead?

GEORGE: Oh, sorry. You can go now, Guys.

(They all break freezes and exit, groaning at the discomfort of holding the freeze, saying things like, "Finally," and "Take your time George." He ignores them, lost in his discouragement.)

JESSICA *(sighs, puts her arm around George):* George. I don't want to keep putting you down. I like how excited you get about stuff. But to be real honest—I just don't think that a play all by itself is going to convert anyone. People have to be looking for God before they find him, and they need to see some of this stuff happening in real life before they're gonna believe it.

GEORGE *(after a long pause):* You're right. . . . But Jess; wouldn't it be good if you really could write a play that would bring people to God?

JESSICA: Yeah, it really would.

(They begin to exit L when a faint sound of singing stops them, the kind of choir singing they used for angels in old movies. It grows louder).

JESSICA: What's that?

(The volume of the singing lowers as God's voice also comes over the sound system.)

GOD'S VOICE: George.

(They both look up.)

GEORGE *(overawed):* Is that you Lord?

GOD'S VOICE: Yes. Don't be discouraged, George, because I have found all your plays pleasing.

GEORGE: Wow. Thank You.

GOD'S VOICE: But George, you don't need to write a play to convert people.

GEORGE: But Father, I really want people to see what you're like.

GOD'S VOICE: Listen, you are my child and you know Me. Your life tells its own story. The light in you will draw people to me.

(George bows his head as the singing dies away. Jessica stares up, then at George, then smiles, then laughs.)

JESSICA: Very cute, George.

GEORGE *(still staring up in awe):* Huh?

JESSICA *(still thinking as she speaks):* Cute . . . I mean, it was all at my expense, but it really is smart. A play within a play. How long did you have this planned? Did you tell everyone else you were gonna do this? Man, you sure predicted my reactions right.

GEORGE: What?

JESSICA: I had no idea. I mean, I really thought you were just floundering around trying out all these dumb ideas, and you've got the whole thing in control all along, all building up to this. *(She gestures up.)* Yeah. Yeah, I think it will work. I mean, we'll cut down on all the dialogue between the scenes, of course.

GEORGE: Jess, I didn't—

JESSICA *(smiling, shaking her head):* God's voice. Well, it's sure been done before, but I think it's a great idea. It really makes that final point that you don't just perform your beliefs, but it doesn't preach. . . . You gave yourself a heck of a pat on the back, but that's . . .

GEORGE *(trying harder to get her attention):* Jessica, please . . .

JESSICA: You know, my only reservation is whether we can keep people with us through those three skits. I mean, they're so lame.

GEORGE *(grabbing her by the shoulders):* Jess—listen. You don't understand. That, that wasn't me!

JESSICA: Well I know that. You could never make your voice that deep. It must have been Alan. *(Calling offstage.)* Hey, Alan, come here.

(She exits in search of Alan.)

GEORGE *(calling after her):* Jessica! *(He looks after her, then gets an idea, thinks for a moment, than looks back up at God.)*

GEORGE: Uh, Lord?

GOD'S VOICE: Yes?

GEORGE: Um, I was thinking; if we all came on stage in the last scene holding sticks, and You turned them all into snakes like You did for Moses and Aaron, that would convince tons of people that You are real. Then You could change them back again before anyone got bit. What do you think?

GOD'S VOICE: No, George.

GEORGE: OK.

(George smiles up at God, then exits.)

Questions for Discussion

1. What were some positive things about George?

2. What were some positive things about Jessica?

3. What was it about each of George's three play ideas that didn't work?

4. What attitude towards Christians do kids at your school have? Is it cool to be a Christian or not?

5. Have you ever tried to tell someone what it's like to be a Christian? How did the conversation go?

6. How can you get the truth about Jesus across to your friends and family who don't believe in Him, without preaching?

How Do You Deal With That?

In these three skits, kids who have decided to live by Christian values struggle with peer pressure to go against their beliefs. The conversations are not conclusive, but aimed at starting discussion on how Christians can stand up for what they believe without losing their friends or coming across as self-righteous.

Cast

Skit One—Leo, a Christian, and his friends Joe and Pete.

Skit Two—Patty, a Christian, and her friends Shannon and Jean.

Skit Three—Andre, a Christian, and Melissa, a confident, attractive girl.

Costumes

All characters can wear ordinary, casual clothes.

Production Notes

These are very simple skits and no props are needed. Actors can remain standing. Unlike some of the scenes in this book, they need to be followed up with discussion to serve any purpose. Discussion would be most effective if you immediately followed each skit with discussion about that skit rather than waiting till the end to discuss all three.

Skit One—On Being a Christian

Leo enters and addresses the audience before the scene begins.

LEO: How do you deal with it when you've got these friends and you've known each other since you were in kindergarten, but now you're a Christian, and they're not? You start going in really different directions, for example, you believe in God, and they believe in *(thinks)* fake IDs; but you still like them and you want to fit in with them, but they keep giving you a hard time? How do you deal with that?

(Joe and Pete enter, Leo greets them.)

LEO: So, what's goin' on?

JOE: Not much. Where have you been all week?

LEO: I went to this camp.

PETE: Church camp?

LEO: Yeah.

PETE *(not impressed):* Hmm.

LEO: It was pretty cool. We swam a lot and went horseback riding and stuff. I met some neat people.

JOE: Did you do religious stuff?

LEO: Yeah. They had speakers and music. But they weren't boring or anything.

PETE: My mom used to make me go to those things. I quit. I don't like all that Sunday school junk. Always telling you what you can't do.

LEO: It wasn't like that. You should come sometime and see.

JOE: Oh yeah. Right.

LEO: Seriously. It's not what you think.

JOE: You gotta get with the times Leo. We grew out of that stuff.

LEO: You Guys, it's not like we sit around singing baby songs. We talk about important stuff.

PETE *(to Joe):* Oh, now he's more important than us because he's got religion.

LEO: I didn't say that!

JOE *(moving to exit):* Better not take him to any parties, he'll call the cops on us.

PETE *(going along with Joe):* He doesn't go to parties. He only goes to prayer meetings. *(Shouts and waves his hands in the air, mocking.)* Hallelujah!

LEO: Come on, you guys.

(They keep laughing as they deliver the next lines and exit.)

JOE: Maybe he'll be a preacher on TV when he grows up.

PETE: Or one of those dudes on the street corners yelling about the end of the world.

LEO *(watching after them, then addressing the audience):* How do you deal with that?

Skit Two—About Sex

Patty enters and addresses the audience before the scene begins.

PATTY: How do you deal with it when all your friends think it's totally OK to have sex with your boyfriend, but you think it is wrong? I mean, how do you tell them about how God meant it to be, without them thinking you're a prude *(or a similar word)*? How do you deal with that?

(Shannon and Jean enter, talking confidentially.)

SHANNON *(to Jean):* So what did he say?

JEAN: Well, I told him I didn't think I knew him well enough— yet! *(They giggle.)*

SHANNON: So, when are you gonna know him well enough?

JEAN: I don't know. At least a month or two I guess. I mean, I don't want him to think I'm one of those girls who just jumps into bed with anyone.

SHANNON: I know. It's hard to know what to do. I mean, I'm afraid John's gonna lose interest in me pretty soon if I don't do it.

33

(Patty approaches them and they all greet each other.)

SHANNON: We were just talking about sex.

JEAN: What's new, huh.

PATTY: So what about it?

JEAN: Well, we were talking about how it's hard to know what you should do. You don't want to be a sleaze or anything, but no one really thinks you should wait till you're married anymore.

PATTY: Well . . .

SHANNON: I mean, of course you've got to really love him and he must really love you.

JEAN: Well sure.

PATTY: I know people who really love each other and don't have sex.

SHANNON: Barbie and Ken, right?

PATTY: No, seriously.

SHANNON: Are they hung up about it or something?

PATTY: No, they're not. They just want to wait till they're married. There's nothing wrong with that.

JEAN: Wait a minute. Do you think you're supposed to wait till you get married?

PATTY: Well, yeah.

SHANNON: Are you serious?

PATTY: Yeah! There's a lot of good reasons to wait till you're married. Plus it's just what I believe.

SHANNON: But you probably won't get married for years!

JEAN: Really. You can't expect to do nothing for all that time. Nobody's gonna put up with that. I wouldn't.

PATTY: Well, if he is a Christian he's gonna agree with me about waiting.

SHANNON: Don't hold your breath.

34

JEAN *(beginning to exit):* Patty, you're a sweetheart, but I think you need to get a life.

(Jean and Shannon begin talking confidentially again as they exit.)

PATTY *(looking after them, shaking her head, then addressing the audience):* How do you deal with that?

Skit Three—On Partying

Andre enters and addresses the audience before the scene begins.

ANDRE: How do you deal with it when you get invited to a party by an awesome person, and you know that everyone in the world is going to be at this party, but you also know what people are gonna be drinking and stuff, and it's gonna get pretty wild, and you know there's no way your parents would want you there and you know you shouldn't be there anyway? I mean, how do you get the nerve to say "no," and even if you do, how do you say it without looking like a complete moron? How do you deal with that?

(Melissa enters, sees Andre and approaches him. Andre is pretty excited about this. Her manner is slightly flirty at first. He's a little flustered.)

MELISSA: Andre, how come you're standing here all alone?

ANDRE: Oh, uh, just kind of happened, I guess.

MELISSA: Usually you've got about five girls hanging around you.

ANDRE: Huh. I wish.

MELISSA: You do? I guess you're already taking someone to the party?

ANDRE: Party? What party?

MELISSA: Come on. The party. Don't tell me you haven't heard about it.

ANDRE: Oh, the one at Ben's place. Oh yeah, I heard someone talking about it.

MELISSA: Everyone's talking about it. You must be spending too much time in the library or something. You should have more fun. So, are you taking someone?

ANDRE: Uh, well, I wasn't really planning to . . .

MELISSA: Wanna take me?

ANDRE *(torn):* Oh wow. *(Aside.)* She wants me to take her. I don't believe this. *(To Melissa.)* That would be so cool . . .

MELISSA: Oh yeah. It's gonna be great.

ANDRE: So everybody's gonna be there, huh?

MELISSA: You know what Ben's like. He'll probably have two bathtubs full of beer and 75 gate-crashers.

ANDRE: Is that right?

MELISSA: And his big brother's gonna get some other stuff too.

ANDRE: Really.

MELISSA: So?

ANDRE: Oh Melissa. I would really like to go with you, I mean, thanks for asking, but I, I wasn't planning to go.

MELISSA: Why, have you got something else to do?

ANDRE: Well, no, it's just, uh, well—it just seems like it's gonna be a party where people really—party.

MELISSA *(bewildered by this obvious statement):* . . . Yes.

ANDRE *(finally getting to the point, with difficulty):* Well, what I mean is, I'm not into drinking or smoking pot or anything and I just decided to stay away from places where people were into it.

MELISSA: Andre, everybody's going. You don't have to do anything. Do you think someone's gonna pin you down and stuff coke up your nose or something?

ANDRE: Well, no! But you know how it is. You get there, and

you feel like a jerk if you're the only one without a drink in your hand.

MELISSA: You know it's a scientific fact that holding a beer never killed anyone.

ANDRE: I know. I just. . . . *(Giving up in frustration.)* Oh, I just can't explain it.

MELISSA *(amused, a little sarcastic):* Well I didn't mean to throw you into major confusion or anything. I think I can probably find someone else to take me.

(She exits. Andre watches after her longingly.)

ANDRE: I'm sure you can. *(To audience.)* Ohhh—how do you deal with that?

Questions for Discussion

Skit One—On Being a Christian

1. How does Leo feel about his friends?

2. How are his friends treating him?

3. How do you think Leo feels in this skit, especially at the end?

4. Have you ever been picked on or made fun of for what you believe?

5. What do you think Leo should do about how his friends are treating him?

Skit Two—About Sex

1. What percentage of kids you know do you think are having sex? How do you think it is affecting them?

2. The Bible is really clear about waiting until you're married to have sex. Brainstorm all the reasons you can think of why God might have set it up that way.

3. How is the pressure to have sex different for guys and girls? Do you think there's a double standard for guys and girls? How do you feel about that? *(Point out that for Christians the command not to have sex before marriage applies equally to men and women.)*

4. What attitudes to guys and relationships were Jean and Shannon showing in the skit? How do you feel about their attitudes?

5. What would you have said to explain your beliefs about sex if you were Patty?

Skit Three—On Partying

1. How was Andre feeling in the skit? Have you ever felt that kind of conflict within yourself?

2. What are your family's rules for where you go and how late you stay out? Do you agree with your parents on this?

3. What are some reasons for staying away from parties where kids are drinking and doing other drugs?

4. If you were in Andre's position, what would you have said to Melissa to explain why you weren't going?

5. Is it harder to stand up to peer pressure from the opposite sex? How do you think people react to someone who has strong values and sticks to them without being self-righteous?

Miracle Rap

This is a rap about Jesus. Rap is one of the main art forms for many American kids so it makes sense to use it to get the gospel across. In this rap, three miracle stories are told, with introductory and concluding verses framing the piece. The audience is involved by reading signs before and after each story.

Cast

Narrator(s)—One or more people with really good rhythm and timing, and strong delivery. The narrator(s) do the rap.

Sign Bearer—Someone to hold up the signs and lead the audience in responding.

Others—Other people can be used in two capacities:
1. To play percussion instruments if you use them.
2. To choreograph some moves and act out the three miracle stories if you choose to do so. If you do act out the stories, you will need the same person to play Jesus in all three scenes. You will also need a male to play a demon-possessed person, a paralyzed person and two friends. At least four other people should play the crowd in each story.

Costumes

You can wear casual clothes or go for a more coordinated look with matching jackets, or even whole outfits like the guys in rap groups. If you act out the stories, you can put Jesus in a pale robe and everyone else in the scenes in darker clothing.

Production Notes

How you perform the rap depends entirely on how many performers you have, what kind of accompaniment you get, and how involved you want to make it.

You can provide your own accompaniment with clapping, snapping and percussion instruments. The audience can join in by snapping in time with a leader. *(Don't have the audience clap; it's too loud and drowns out the words.)* If you have someone good on electronic keyboard, you could get him to custom-make a tape, or even better, play it live. You can also hunt down a commercial accompaniment tape of rap music without lyrics and find a piece that fits to the rap. Take care not to pick music that is too fast or the words will be lost by the audience, and the action will go by too quickly.

Another choice you have is to choreograph some moves to the rap, and/or you can act out the three miracle stories. If you want people to watch the stories being acted out, don't have too much movement going on at the same time or the audience will be distracted. Narrators can be part of the action or rap from the sidelines. *(If you want to make things really simple, just have kids take turns narrating the rap and moving however they like.)*

Stage directions in the script give you some ideas and timing suggestions. You can leave a line of space after each line delivered in the story sections of the rap if you want to give your actors more time to act out the stories.

Before you begin the rap, you should introduce it and tell the audience you want them to be a part of it. Get the sign bearer to explain that they are to read the sign whenever he holds it up, and rehearse that with both signs. Warn them to be watching out for the signs and place the signbearer to one side of the stage, prominent but not in front of any of the action.

The Script

Music starts as Narrators enter and begin the rap.

We're here today on a special mission
Playin' our part in the great commission
To tell you 'bout the Man whose life does please us
Tell you 'bout the Man whose name is Jesus.

The stories we tell will get you snappin'
These are stories that really happened
If you got a mind not to believe us
Check out the source before you leave us.

Jesus was born in Bethlehem, *(You could refer to a Bible.)*
To Mary his mother and God, not man
He was the one who God had sent to
Show us to live like we were meant to.

The Gospel of Mark is where we're lookin'
To see what the life of Jesus took in
We'll tell you which verses and you're invited
To check them out if you get excited.

(Talk, don't rap the next two lines to the audience.) OK, you
all ready for some wild stories?

Audience Sign: Yeah!

(People acting out the scene get quickly into place.)

(Still talking.) OK, here we go . . . Mark—one—verse—
twenty-one *(Rap again.)*

Jesus starts preachin' in Galilee
(Jesus stands on something, others face him.)
Tellin' people how He can set them free
(Jesus mimes preaching.)
In comes a man with an evil spirit
(One of the crowd steps out, staggers, falls to the ground.)
Jesus can tell soon as He gets near it.
(Jesus moves toward him.)

The demon through the man screams out
(Man mimes screaming.)
Jesus not phased says "Hush, get out!"
(Jesus points down at him in a commanding manner.)
The crowd says "Who can this man be

(Man sits up, crowd is amazed and speaks the line too.)
To have so much authority?"
(Crowd speaks the line too, addressing each other.)

Audience sign: Wow!

(Aside to audience): Don't be callin' no ghostbusters when it's Jesus you're gonna need.

(Addressing audience): OK, you ready for another story.

Audience sign: Yeah!

(People acting out the scene get quickly into place.)

(Addressing audience): Well here it comes . . . Mark—two—verse—number—one. *(Rap again.)*

Back in His hometown the news gets loud
(Crowd gathers, backs to audience.)
So Jesus gives the word to a packed in crowd
(Crowd is smashed together.)
Space is so tight that the people can't move
(Crowd squirms against each other.)
All of a sudden there's a hole in the roof.
(All at once, they all look up.)

Down comes a man in a paralyzed state
(Crowd parts to either side to reveal a person being lowered to the floor by two friends.)
Carried by his friends whose faith is great
(They lay him on the ground and look at Jesus.)
Jesus makes him well like they knew he would be
(Jesus touches him and he stands up.)
Crowd is amazed and so they should be.
(Crowd looks amazed.)

Audience sign: Wow!

(Aside to audience): If Jesus can do that for him He can even work with you.

(To audience): OK, get set for the third story . . . Mark—four—verse—thirty-five. *(Rap again.)*

Jesus and His men go out in a boat
(Crowd sits as if in a boat, rocking back and forth. Jesus is lying down in front.)
A storm comes up and it's hard to float
(Rocking gets more violent.)
Disciples start to whine and scream and cry
(Crowd whines, screams, cries.)
"Wake up Lord—we're gonna die!"
(Crowd speaks the line too.)

Jesus doesn't see the need to worry
(Jesus stands up calmly.)
Shouts "Be still" and calms the flurry
(Mimes or shouts the line, arms raised.)
Waves that heaved and crashed and roared
(Crowd stops rocking and looks out at the sea, stunned)
Stopped and peace was soon restored.
(Crowd looks at each other, stunned.)

The men were shocked down to their bones
(Crowd shakes their heads in wonder.)
Talked in low and awe-struck tones
(Crowd whispers to each other.)
"Who's this man that storms can't sway Him
(Crowd says the line too.)
Even the wind and the waves obey Him!"
(Crowd says the line too.)

Audience sign: Wow!

(Aside to audience): This is not a man to mess with we're dealin' with here.

(To audience): OK, you got ears open for the finish?

Audience sign: Yeah!

Well here it is then. *(Rap again.)*

As you can see from this excursion
Jesus is no ordinary person
Folks who think He's just a great teacher
Close their eyes to the God-like features.

He's so great He can juggle with planets
Flatten out mountains of solid granite
Think you can live without His direction?
Try pullin' off your own resurrection.

(Aside to audience): You know what I'm sayin don't you?
He who has ears, let him hear.

There's good news for the human race
God is big on love and grace
Jesus did miracles to get our attention
Savin' our lives is His main intention.

The rap we've done is to get the word out
Sometimes in life the truth gets blurred out
The utmost important thing to do
Is let Jesus make a miracle out of you.

(All point to the audience and cut the music right on "you.")

Questions for Discussion

1. What did Jesus do in the three stories that were in the rap?

2. What do these stories tell us about what Jesus is like?

3. Do you think Jesus is still doing miracles in people's lives today?

4. Do you have any stories of how Jesus has acted in your life?

That Sin

In this scene a person's struggle and escape from a sinful habit is illustrated. The message of the scene is that a private struggle of personal will does not set us free, and that we need to surrender to God's power and obey His command of confession. Because of the abstract nature of the scene, a brief introduction is included in the script.

Cast

Person—A male or female who is good at using body language and facial expressions to show feelings.

That Sin—A swift, graceful, evil character, male or female.

Jesus—A confident, natural actor.

Costumes

That Sin can wear a red T–shirt with "That Sin" written on it. Jesus can wear a white T–shirt with "Jesus" written on it. The Person can wear ordinary casual clothes.

Production Notes

The only prop you need is a stool placed C. If you have lights, it would be good to dim them at the point where the Person exits with That Sin, and to bring them up stronger than they were at the beginning at the point where Jesus enters.

In this play, even more than most, movement is very important. Where actors stand, walk, and sit should be worked on carefully. Movement and expression will convey feelings more than the dialogue.

The mood of the scene is slightly comical at first, becoming more serious as the depth of the Person's shame and defeat is revealed.

If you want to avoid having people making the automatic association that the sin is sexual, you should probably avoid casting a male as The Person with a female as That Sin.

Before the drama begins an announcer comes out and introduces the play.

ANNOUNCER: This is a scene about a person fighting against a sin. We're not saying which sin because everyone struggles with different sins, and we want the scene to speak to you. The character in the play named That Sin could represent a lot of things. It might be a habit like lying or losing your temper. It might be a drinking problem or a sexual sin. It might be a private thing that only goes on in your head, like thinking evil thoughts about someone. Whatever it is, That Sin stands for something you know is wrong and want to stop doing, but can't stop. *(He exits.)*

(Person enters, looking troubled. He sits on the stool and talks to himself.)

PERSON: I've decided. I've finally decided. I've just got to stop. I don't care how hard it is. I'm never going to do it again. I'm not even going to think about it, because every time I think about that sin, I end up doing it, so I just won't think about it. Nope. No way. . . . Here I am, not thinking about it. Doing good, doing good . . .

(He breaks off as his eye catches That Sin, who enters, crosses in front of the stool and exits out the other side. The Person's gaze follows That Sin the whole time. Then he shakes his head, as if to snap out of it, gets up and starts pacing, frustrated.)

PERSON: Oh! I thought about it again. Bummer! Well, I was just getting it out of my system. That's it now.

(He glances over to where That Sin exited. That Sin peeks her head on stage, grins, waves and disappears as the Person once again tears his gaze away, exasperated.)

PERSON *(groans):* Why do I do that! I don't want to think about it! I don't want to live like this any more. . . . It's messing up the rest of my life. I don't even understand why I like it. I must be crazy or something. Well, not any more. That's it. It's over. It's finished.

(He stands straight, looking determined. He crosses his arms with resolution. Meanwhile, That Sin has reentered from behind, and creeps up on him, getting very close, then jumping in front of him. Taken off guard, he jerks his head back, but his gaze is arrested and he stares, helpless as That Sin circles around him, holding his gaze. That Sin begins to back towards the exit, beckoning to him. With great effort, he tears his eyes away and yells.)

PERSON: No!

(That Sin shrugs and leaves. The Person, shaken, sits back on the stool, runs his hands through his hair.)

PERSON: Why does it keep coming back on me? I don't want it, I know it's wrong. I feel like scum after I do it! . . . I don't think it's ever going to leave me alone.

(As soon as he says the last line, That Sin takes a running leap on stage and with great enjoyment throws herself in front of the Person, who turns away, but That Sin keeps up a game of just beating the Person to every place he turns, and being right there when he opens his eyes. If the person playing That Sin has any dance or gymnastics training, you could make this section really active, with That Sin pursuing the Person all over the stage, spinning or tumbling or whatever. Finally the Person yells, louder than before.)

PERSON: Leave me alone!

(That Sin smiles and leaves.)

PERSON *(shaken):* This is harder than I thought. I always thought I could quit if I really wanted to. I've got to get a grip. I just need to stay logical about this and use some willpower. The fact is, it's wrong, I hate it, it was a mistake to ever get started. I mean, it does feel good for a while, I'll admit it. But it's not worth it. Just because something feels good. . . . *(Thinks.)* Actually it feels great. . . .*(Thinks some more, smiles.)* Actually I don't think I'm ever going to find anything that feels that good.

(Suddenly, That Sin rushes on and stops cold, standing right next to him, confident. The Person stares, making no move to get away, but he looks really alarmed.)

PERSON: What are you doing here.

THAT SIN: You invited me.

PERSON: I did not. Go away. *(He doesn't say it with much energy.)*

THAT SIN: Yeah you did. You were just thinking about how great it was when you were with me and you wished it would happen again. So here I am.

PERSON *(half-heartedly):* Go away.

THAT SIN *(smiling, touching him):* Do you really want me to?

(That Sin reaches out her hand. Slowly, reluctantly, the Person takes it. That Sin, holding his gaze, leads him off-stage. After a pause, the Person reenters, despondent. He sits and buries his face in his hands in despair. Jesus enters and says his name.)

JESUS *(gently):* What happened?

(Person starts, sees Jesus and turns away in shame. He shakes his head but can't speak.)

JESUS: Look at me.

PERSON: I can't.

JESUS: Why.

PERSON: I did it again. I always do. How can I say I believe in you? I feel like a hypocrite . . . I can't change.

JESUS: That's true.

PERSON *(glances quickly at him, then down again):* I tried to be a Christian.

JESUS: What?

PERSON *(rising and moving away from him):* I really tried.

JESUS *(moving towards him):* Wait. Do you think you're not a Christian because you keep falling into this sin?

PERSON *(finally turning toward him):* How can I be?

JESUS: How can't you be?

PERSON: I just can't fight any more. I don't have anything left to fight with.

JESUS: Then stop it.

(The Person gives him a questioning look.)

JESUS: Do you want to be free of this?

PERSON: Of course.

JESUS *(taking his shoulder):* Will you do anything?

PERSON: Yes!

JESUS: Then start living the way I told you to.

PERSON: I tried!

JESUS: Yes, you tried. You try when you need to be giving up. You grit your teeth when you should be calling me.

PERSON: I'm doing everything I know how to do!

JESUS: What are you supposed to do about sin?

PERSON: Stop it.

JESUS: What else.

PERSON: I don't know.

JESUS: Yes you do. The verse is in your head right now.

PERSON *(rolling his eyes in defeat):* Confess. I do. I'm always confessing to you.

JESUS: You confess to the air. You don't come to me.

PERSON *(after a pause):* I'm too ashamed.

JESUS: And?

PERSON *(sighs):* Too proud.

JESUS: No one who can't confess to another person can get close to confessing to me.

PERSON *(alarmed):* Someone else! I can't tell anyone! I thought we were allowed to come right to you!

JESUS: Speak out the verse that's in your head.

PERSON *(reluctant):* Confess your sins to one another and pray for one another.

JESUS: . . . So that you might be healed.

PERSON: That's too hard. No one knows this about me. Nobody. It would blow them away.

JESUS: Do you want to be free of this?

PERSON: Of course.

JESUS: Will you do anything to be free of this?

PERSON *(very upset):* I can't do that!

(He moves away from Jesus. They look at each other for a moment. Jesus looks sad. Slowly he takes a few steps away. From the other side of the stage, That Sin reenters and approaches the Person. Against his will, the Person begins to look at her, and to lean towards her. He is in a lot of pain. That Sin starts to lead him away. At first he follows reluctantly, but then he tears himself away and cries out.)

PERSON: Jesus!

(Immediately, Jesus moves between Person and That Sin, pushing That Sin away and putting his arm around the Person, who leans on him and buries his face in his shoulder. That Sin narrows her eyes and reluctantly backs away and exits.)

PERSON *(shaken):* OK. I'll do it. I'll tell people and face whatever happens. *(Looking at Jesus.)* I'm scared.

JESUS: I know.

PERSON: Will you come with me?

JESUS: Of course. I'll never leave you.

(They exit together.)

Questions for Discussion

1. What are some sins people struggle with which turn into habits or addictions?

2. How do you feel when you really want to change the way you act, but you keep failing?

3. How was the guy trying to fight the sin at the beginning of the play, before Jesus came on? *(Answer—in his own power.)*

4. What did Jesus say he had to do? *(Answer—Surrender the problem to Him, asking for His help, and obeying His command to confess our sins to one another.)*

5. Who can you talk to about things in your life that you struggle with and are ashamed of? Do you confess your sins to someone or do you keep them to yourself?

6. What can we do to help each other live free of sin? *(Some ideas: Don't tempt each other, confront someone in love if you see them doing wrong, don't condemn people for their sins, be very careful to keep information confidential if someone confesses a sin to you.)*

The Boring Youth Group

In this scene a group of totally bored young people go through a radical change when they start to serve people, study the Bible and pray. Using simple comedy and natural dialogue, the scene challenges people to stop waiting to be entertained and start following Jesus. Techniques of mime, freezing action and addressing the audience directly are used to keep the play light and fast-paced. This is a good scene for using lots of kids in performing. The parts are not too demanding, but the timing of the piece is important so it needs to be well-rehearsed.

Cast

The narrator can be a young person or an adult. This part requires good speaking ability and good comic timing. Besides narration, the scene has speaking parts which can be divided up any way you choose among anywhere from 6 to 20 or more kids. When the same person speaks more than once, their number in the margin will just be repeated. Otherwise, numbers go in sequence and you can designate the lines any way you want, except that there are a few times where males or females are specified.

Kids can be themselves or adopt a character if they choose. People with more interest or more time available can be designated more lines.

Costumes

Performers wear whatever they would normally wear to youth group, or dress as any character they want to portray.

Production Notes

Because a lot of the action is mimed, there is little need for props. All you will need are a few Bibles, and some steps or blocks which put performers on different levels so you can see them all when they stand in a group.

The Script

Youth group enters and gathers center stage, as if posed for a photograph. Narrator stands or sits to one side of the stage.

NARRATOR: Once, there was a church youth group.

(Altogether, they wave and say "Hi" to the audience.)

NARRATOR: This youth group was full of great kids . . .

(Altogether, they nod, say "It's true," and then pat one another on the back.)

NARRATOR: However, in spite of this, the fact is, it was a boring youth group.

(Altogether, they nod, say "Boring," then look at a few surrounding people and repeat "Boring," nodding to one another in agreement.)

NARRATOR: A lot of these people really did want to be part of a youth group . . .

LINE 1 *(moving to the front of the group to address the audience):* I need to be in a youth group. Ever since I became a Christian last year I've wanted to get to know kids at church. A lot of kids at school are pressuring me to do stuff that's wrong, so I need to have other friends.

NARRATOR: On the other hand, others were dragged to youth group by their parents and would rather be cleaning their grandparents' basement or watching the weather channel.

LINE 2 *(moving to the front of the group to address the audience):* I'd be outa here in a second if my parents hadn't threatened to ground me if I don't come. What's the point of being here if I hate it? I'm old enough to make up my own mind about who I hang out with.

NARRATOR: And, some of them had ulterior motives for being there.

LINE 3 *(a guy):* The main attraction here for me is definitely— girls. I come to check out the babes. *(Or whatever guys in your area call girls.)*

NARRATOR: In spite of all these differences, they all had one opinion in common.

ALL: This is boring.

(All yawn and sit down as Narrator continues.)

NARRATOR: The youth sponsors *(or whatever you call adult leaders)* had tried everything to keep them amused. They had played every game in the fat, lime green and purple book titled *"Super-Whammy Games to Bring Boring Youth Groups to Life."*

LINE 4 *(a girl, standing while she speaks, hands on hips):* I swear, if we play any more dumb games I'm going to gag. I mean seriously, how long can you go around making animal noises, or stumbling through mazes blindfolded. Like, what will they do next? Bury us alive and see who can dig out first? Please.

NARRATOR: And not only had they played all the games, they had gone everywhere you could imagine. There was nowhere left to go.

(The next section of dialogue builds in volume and intensity to climax at the last "Done that." People delivering the lines offering suggestions will stand up to address the group, and be dragged back down by whoever is sitting around them as the suggestion is rejected.)

LINE 5: Let's go to a baseball game.

ALL: Been there.

LINE 6: Let's go skating.

ALL: Done that.

LINE 7: Let's go to the zoo.

ALL: Been there.

LINE 8: Let's go bowling.

ALL: Done that.

LINE 9: Let's go *(to the nearest amusement park)*.

ALL: Been there.

LINE 10: Let's go camping at *(nearby national forest)*.

ALL: Done that.

LINE 11: Let's go on a safari in Africa.

ALL: Been there.

LINE 12: Let's go bungee jumping over the Grand Canyon!

ALL: Done that.

NARRATOR: After every activity it was still the same story . . .

ALL: We're still bored.

NARRATOR: Things went on like this for a long time, until, one day, someone got an idea.

LINE 13: Hey, I've got an idea!

ALL: What?

LINE 14: Well, we're a church group, so we need to be doing what the Bible says, right?

(Group agrees tentatively, ad-libbing lines like, "Well, yeah.," "I guess so.," etc.)

LINE 14: Well, I was reading in one of the gospels about Jesus, and He was always helping people. He said to feed hungry people and visit sick people and stuff. Maybe we should be into that kind of thing.

LINE 15: Well, I guess we could try it.

LINE 16: Why not. It couldn't be any more boring than what we're doing now.

NARRATOR: So, the next Saturday, they got into smaller groups and went to help different people.

(As Narrator speaks, they all roll up their sleeves and move into three small groups, a little more animated than they have been so far.)

NARRATOR: Some of them went to a soup kitchen and served food . . .

(A small group forms an assembly line SR and begins to mime serving food. One ladles soup, one hands over bread, one pours a drink, etc. They keep going as the narrator continues.)

NARRATOR: Some of them went and cleaned house for an elderly lady who had broken her hip.

(A small group goes SL and begins to mime cleaning, vacuuming, dusting, washing dishes, etc. They also keep going as the narrator continues.)

NARRATOR: Some of them went to the airport to meet a group of international students coming from China. They took them to where they would be staying and then out to lunch.

(The last group moves DSC and mimes shaking hands, talking to imaginary people using big gestures, and carrying suitcases. You could make this quite comical by portraying communication problems in expressions and gestures. They continue until the narrator finishes the next line.)

NARRATOR: When the youth group met later, they all had a lot to talk about.

(All actors freeze. A representative from each of the three small groups comes forward and addresses the audience. After they speak they freeze with their heads down.)

LINE 17 *(from the soup kitchen group):* I never thought working in a soup kitchen was going to be fun. I was grossed out at first; so many people were in really bad shape. But when I started giving out the food and talking, I found out they weren't any different from us. They're just broke. And I felt really good to be helping them out. Like I was doing something that mattered and not just staying in my safe neighborhood taking care of myself.

LINE 18 *(from the cleaning group):* I can't believe I've always lived so close to that lady without getting to know her. She's really sweet. When we told her we wanted to clean for her, she was so grateful she started to cry. She's in one of those walker things and she couldn't bend down to clean. It was driving her crazy but she didn't have the money to hire anyone. I'm really glad we did that. We're going to go back and help her once a week. She gave us each a little ornament to say thanks.

LINE 19 *(from the airport group):* I didn't know if I'd hit it off with Chinese people. I was afraid we wouldn't understand each other at all, or they'd act really bizarre and I'd get all embarrassed. But they were neat, and we didn't have any problems talking. The funny thing was, I thought we were just going to be helping these guys out, but we learned all kinds of stuff from them. They're really sharp. They said when they get settled in they want to have us over for Chinese food. I could go for that.

(Actors break freeze and all exit.)

NARRATOR: Since doing things for people who need help seemed to work out so well, the youth group decided to check out what else the Bible had to say.

LINE 20 *(actor carries on a ladder, places it USC and climbs up it):* You wouldn't believe the stuff in the Bible. You read it, and realize God's been trying to get our attention for centuries. He's always looking out for people, always watching over us.

(He freezes in a position of leaning forward, looking over the downstage area, concerned.)

LINE 21 *(a girl, speaking as she enters and stopping SR):* I didn't think God would forgive me for the things I've done until I heard the story of the woman at the well. *(She mimes as she continues to speak, taking a bucket, tying it to a rope, then lowering it into a well, and bringing it back up again.)* There was an outcast woman getting water from a well in the heat of the day, when no one else would be around. Jesus came to the well and broke the rules and talked to her. *(Stop movement to show a surprised reaction to Jesus.)* He told her about God. Then, so that she'd believe in Him, He went on to tell her that He knew she'd had five husbands and was living with a different man right then. He knew everything she'd ever done, but He found her, and talked with her anyway. *(She freezes in some motion, with an expression of focus on Jesus.)*

LINE 22 *(a boy enters, running, stops DSC and mimes the movements he describes in the following):* I think the story of David is really cool. He had so much faith that God was going to help him that he went into a fight with this giant, killer of a guy, and he got him with just a slingshot. He won. I want to have that kind of guts, to be able to fight whatever God wants me to fight. *(He freezes in a position where he is looking down with his hands on the hips, as though surveying Goliath on the ground.)*

LINE 23 *(a girl enters, and stops SL):* I didn't used to think I was ever going to be able to change my life. I thought I was stuck with my problems and that's all there was to it. But I heard a story that showed me that Jesus will change you when you can't change yourself. There was a lady who had some awful health problems. She was always bleeding and had spent all she had on doctors and nothing helped. When she heard Jesus was coming, she pushed her way through to Him *(She mimes what she is describing.)* and just touched His clothes. The bleeding stopped. She was so used to being ashamed, that she didn't even want Him to notice her. But He stopped and asked who touched Him. She fell down on her knees, so scared she was shaking. But He told her that her faith had healed her and she was free of her suffering. *(She freezes, still on her knees, looking up at Jesus.)*

(For a few seconds, all four actors remain still, then they melt out of the freezes and quietly exit.)

NARRATOR: After they had been studying the Bible for a while, they decided to start praying together too.

(In the next section, there is a rhythm to the dialogue. The same person who says line 24 will pray the Lord's Prayer, but others will expound on its meaning. The lines should flow together, almost overlapping, punctuated by a line being repeated by all before the prayer continues. During the recitation, the group will be filtering back on stage and assembling in their original positions. Actors enter just before they say their first line, so if you have a big group, you don't have to have them all on stage until toward the end of the prayer. In this case, when the script specifies "All" it means all the people on stage so far. How you order and choreograph this section will depend on how many actors you have.)

LINE 24 *(moving to an elevated and central position):* We started praying the Lord's prayer together, instead of just rattling it off in church. I didn't know it meant anything. Now it means so much to me I feel like I'm in on a huge secret. *(Begins to pray.)* Our Father in heaven, hallowed be your name . . .

LINE 25: Our Father

LINE 26: Our Dad

LINE 27: My Dad

LINE 28: My Dad who always hears me

LINE 29: My Dad who always sees me

LINE 30: My Dad who wouldn't ever leave me

ALL: Holy be your name.

LINE 24: Your kingdom come, your will be done
on earth as it is in heaven.

LINE 31: Your kingdom come

LINE 32: Your love

LINE 33: Your power

LINE 34: Your truth

LINE 35: Your plans for us

ALL: Come

LINE 36: Come to our church

LINE 37: Come to our families

LINE 38: Come to our friends

LINE 39: Come to our school

LINE 40: Come into our spirits

ALL: On earth as it is in heaven.

LINE 24: Give us today our daily bread.

LINE 41: Give us everything we need, so we will think about you instead.

LINE 42: Give us only what we need, so nothing else gets in your way

ALL: Give us today our daily bread.

LINE 24: Forgive us our debts, as we also have forgiven our debtors.

LINE 43: Forgive us for what we can never make up for

LINE 44: The things we've done in the dark

LINE 45: The things we've done with our hate

LINE 46: The needs we've ignored

LINE 47: Forgive us or we can't go on

ALL: And we will forgive each other.

LINE 24: And lead us not into temptation, but deliver us from the evil one.

LINE 48: Lead us not into temptation

LINE 49: Don't let us get sucked under

LINE 50: Keep us safe in the longings that tear us apart

LINE 51: Protect us from the lies we want to believe

LINE 52: Save us from the one who wants us to die young

ALL: Deliver us from the evil one.

LINE 24: For yours is the kingdom and the power and the glory forever. Amen.

(The group repeats the final lines in a three part round, a total of three times. The volume builds each time. The second group should start after the first group says "kingdom" and the third group starts after the first group says "glory." While waiting for the whole group to catch up, the second and third groups should repeat "Amen." The last "Amen" should be the loudest, and then they stop sharply and freeze as the narrator speaks.)

NARRATOR *(after a pause):* Not too long after the youth group decided to help people, to study the Bible, and to pray, they realized something.

LINE 53 *(addressing the rest of the group):* Hey, have you guys noticed something?

LINE 54: Yeah, something's different than it used to be.

LINE 55: I was thinking the same thing. You know what it is?

ALL *(to each other):* We're not bored anymore! *(To audience.)* We're definitely not bored!

(They start talking to one another excitedly and exit quickly in both directions.)

Questions for Discussion

1. What makes a group of people interesting to be around?

2. Why do you think some people are bored a lot even though they do plenty of fun activities?

3. Have any of you ever had a good experience of helping someone else? When? How did you feel?

4. Have any of you ever gotten excited about Bible study or praying? What happened?

5. Is your youth group more like the group was at the beginning of the play or at the end?

6. Are there any changes you would like to see your youth group make? What? What could you do about making that happen?

Double Life

In this scene a high school girl struggles with the conflict between living as a Christian and longing to fit in with a fun crowd at school. Her efforts to live in two worlds lead to a lot of tension and confusion. In the end she realizes that she has to make a choice one way or the other.

Cast

Narrator

Amy—The main character.

Mother—Amy's mother.

Cathy—Amy's best friend at school.

Jeff—A friend who has a bad reputation.

Nathan—A guy who Amy is interested in, Jeff's friend.

Youth Minister

Other youth group members, and possibly extras for the other group at the end of the play. Use between five and ten people for the youth group.

Costumes

Casual clothes are fine for all the characters. Mother will need to wear something that marks her as older; maybe a skirt, with her hair tied back. She should be a realistic mother, not a caricature.

Production Notes

Scenes change a lot in this skit but it can still be kept very simple by having Amy mime using props instead of bothering with real objects. If you have a few chairs or blocks at center stage, they can be used whenever the action calls for sitting.

You will need to make the sound of a phone ringing offstage once, but you can mime the phone. The only props you really need to use are a guitar for one of the youth group members, some Bibles when the youth group comes on a second time, and a school bag with books and a cassette tape in it.

If you have lighting available for your performing space, you could have the center area of the stage set up as Amy's bedroom and have scenes in all other places spotlighted on different areas of the stage. Or, if you have a curtain, you could have the main stage set as a bedroom and close the curtain to do other scenes in front of it. If you would like the play to be more realistic and you do have stage lighting or curtains, you can make a bedroom set and use real props in the bedroom scenes instead of miming.

The Script

Narrator enters and stands to one side of the stage. She remains in the sidelines for most of the play, although you could have her moving onto the stage and walking around during monologues; Amy also enters and stands DC.

NARRATOR *(gesturing to Amy):* This is Amy. Amy is *(Insert what year of school she's in.).* She's popular, does well in school, and has a nice family. However, Amy spends most of her time feeling pretty stressed-out. *(Amy runs her fingers through her hair with a worried expression.)* Her problem is that she can't make up her mind. Sometimes, she wants to live as a Christian, like when she goes to youth group on Sunday night . . .

(Youth group enters and Amy joins them. They sit in a tight semicircle; some people sitting on the floor. The youth leader has a guitar and plays quietly. The others listen or sing along quietly as Narrator continues.)

NARRATOR: People in the youth group are really nice to each other, much nicer than kids at school. They do a lot together;

even things like mission trips to Mexico. When the youth minister talks, it seems to Amy like following Jesus is the only life in the world that makes any sense.

YOUTH MINISTER *(stops playing guitar):* You Guys, Christianity isn't a bunch of rules; it's belonging to Jesus. Jesus is always with you. He's with you when you're brushing your teeth in the morning, He's with you in the hallway at school when everyone is shoving each other and telling gross jokes, He never leaves you . . .

(All freeze as Narrator continues.)

NARRATOR: But there are other times when the last thing Amy wants to think about is how Jesus is always with her. Like most of the time at school . . .

(Amy stands, leaves youth group and drifts to SL as youth group exits. Cathy enters L, in a hurry.)

CATHY: There you are! I was afraid you'd caught your bus home already. Listen, you've gotta come with me.

AMY: Why?

CATHY: Because Jeff just asked me if I want to go over to his place, and guess who's gonna be there too?

AMY *(looking at her watch, then over her shoulder):* Who?

CATHY: Nathan! So stop worrying about your bus. Come on.

AMY *(flustered):* Oh no. You didn't let him know I liked him did you?

CATHY: No, I swear. I was totally cool about it. I just said you were gonna be with me. So come on!

AMY: Oh man, this is neat, but, well, what about Jeff—you know how he's really into partying lately—he wouldn't get us into any trouble would he?

CATHY: Man, Amy, grow up. A few beers never hurt anyone.

AMY: Well, if my parents ever found out . . . I mean, they're gonna ask where I was.

CATHY: Oh, you can think of something to say. Look—your bus is coming. I set this up for you perfectly. You're always saying you never get a chance to talk to him. Are you coming or what?

AMY *(thinks for a few more seconds):* OK—let's do it!

(They exit quickly.)

NARRATOR: When Amy gets with those kids, being a Christian seems impossible. She's sure they would laugh at her if they knew what she believed, so she keeps quiet.

(Jeff, Nathan, Cathy and Amy enter. Cathy and Jeff each have a beer. Nathan has two cans. While Nathan and Amy talk, Cathy and Jeff mime having their own conversation in the background.)

NATHAN: Hey Amy—Whatcha got empty hands for? Here. *(He tosses her a can of beer.)* You know, I used to think you were kind of dull, but you're definitely loosening up. What are you doing this weekend?

AMY: Oh, I don't know. Nothing much.

NATHAN: I drove past *(Give a local supermarket name.)* on Saturday and I saw you with a bunch of people washing cars. What was that all about?

AMY: Oh, that was just some people from my church. We're raising money. *(She seems uncomfortable talking about church.)*

NATHAN: What for?

AMY: Uh, we're going to Mexico.

NATHAN: Really? That's cool. I've always wanted to go there.

AMY: Well it's not like a vacation or anything. We're going down to help build a new room onto an orphanage and teach Bible school to the kids and stuff.

NATHAN *(interested):* That sounds neat.

AMY *(surprised):* It does?

(They all exit, still talking, as Narrator continues.)

NARRATOR: It never occurs to Amy that her friends might be interested in what's going on with her church; she's too worried about what they think of her to wonder what they think about Jesus. So she keeps a double life going without letting one side affect the other. But sometimes it gets confusing . . .

(In the next scene Amy is trying to conduct a phone conversation and lie to her Mother at the same time. Keep it moving quickly so the confusion is believable. Amy is highly emotional throughout the scene. She enters, sits and mimes being at a bedroom dresser, brushing her hair and spraying it. Her mother enters.)

MOTHER: Amy, hurry, we're leaving for church in a minute.

AMY: OK Mom. Who's preaching, do you know?

MOTHER: John, I think.

AMY: Oh good, I like him.

(Mother exits, then the phone rings.)

AMY: I got it! *(She picks up the phone and speaks into it.)* Oh, Nathan. Hi. . . . You're going to the lake. Oh wow. What time? Oh man, I can't make it. I have to go to church with my parents or they'll flip out. . . . It doesn't finish till noon. . . . What? Pick me up from there? . . . Well . . .

(Mother enters.)

MOTHER: Come on, Honey.

AMY *(into the phone):* Just a sec Natha—Nancy. *(To Mother.)* Mom, can I go out right after church? This girl wants me to help her with a science project.

MOTHER: Sure. We can drop you off at her place after lunch.

AMY: No! *(Into the phone)* No Nath-Nancy. I wasn't talking to you. Just a minute. *(To Mother.)* No Mom. She wants to pick me up right from church.

MOTHER: But we always have lunch together after church. Can't you wait till after?

AMY *(urgently)*: Mom! He—she—can't wait! Please?

MOTHER: Amy why are you so frantic about this?

AMY: I'm not! *(Into the phone.)* I mean I am! Yeah, I really want to come. Just a minute. *(To Mother.)* Mom, please! I owe her a favor. She's in a hurry.

MOTHER: Oh, all right. Hurry now. *(She exits.)*

AMY *(into the phone)*: Nancy! I mean Nathan! I'm coming. But don't come right to the church, OK? I'll meet you at the restaurant next door.

(She hangs up, sighs with relief, and exits.)

NARRATOR: As time passes, Amy finds that living in two worlds is getting harder. Sooner or later, someone's going to see through the cracks . . .

(Amy enters with a school bag containing books and a cassette tape. She mimes getting ready for school, checking over the contents of the bag. She pulls out the tape and looks at it. Then her mother enters, calling her. Startled, Amy jumps, and hides the tape behind her back.)

MOTHER: Amy, what's the matter?

AMY: You surprised me!

MOTHER: Well sorry! I just wanted to know if you have lunch money.

AMY: I've got some. I'm fine.

MOTHER *(noting Amy's odd position)*: Honey, what have you got behind your back?

AMY: Nothing.

MOTHER: Then why are you standing there with your arms pinned behind you.

68

AMY: It's nothing Mom.

MOTHER: Now I'm getting curious.

AMY: It's just a tape. No big deal. *(She holds the tape out but covers most of it with her hand.)*

MOTHER: You're the one who's making a big deal out of it. *(She holds out her hand. Amy rolls her eyes nervously and hands it over. Mother reads a title out loud.)*

MOTHER: "Multimegadeth—Out of the Slime Pit and Into Your Soul"? *(or a similar title)* . . . Amy, since when have you liked this kind of music?

AMY: It's not even my tape. Someone gave it to me to give to someone else.

MOTHER: Do their parents know they're listening to this kind of stuff?

AMY: They probably don't care.

MOTHER: Well I do. I can't understand why you would want to listen to this. It goes against what you believe in. You can tell that from just looking at the cover. And you tried to hide it from me, which is just the same as lying.

AMY *(raising her voice):* I think it's my business what music I listen to.

MOTHER: I think we need to talk a lot more about this when you get home from school.

(They look at each other for a few seconds, then exit in opposite directions. As Narrator continues, Amy reenters and sits C with a dejected expression.)

NARRATOR: When Amy's parents found out about some of the things she had been doing, she was grounded for a long time. It gave her a lot of time alone. Whenever Amy has enough time alone to really think about her life, she gets depressed. She used to like being alone, to read, to write in her diary, to pray. She felt close to God back then. Now she doesn't really feel close to anyone, even though she

69

spends so much time with people. She thought about the people at church . . .

(Youth group enters R and stands in a group SR, talking and laughing, a few kids holding Bibles.)

She thought about the people from school . . .

(Cathy, Jeff and Nathan, and possibly others, enter L, talking and laughing, and stand SL. Amy looks from one group to another.)

NARRATOR: . . . And she realized something.

(All freeze except Amy.)

AMY *(thinking out loud):* I'm sick of this. I'm trying to fit in with everyone, but I don't feel like I really belong with anyone. I'm spending so much time faking it, I don't even know who I really am. I don't know if I believe what they believe, *(Looking at the youth group.)* or if I just want to have a good time. *(Looking at the other group, then straight out for the last line.)* I need to make up my mind.

(Amy holds her position for a few seconds, then all break freezes and exit.)

Questions for Discussion

1. What did Amy think about church?

2. What did she like about her friends who weren't involved in church?

3. What are some examples of how Amy was being two-faced?

4. What are some of the feelings of a person who is living a double life?

5. Have any of you ever been like Amy?

6. What do you think Amy should do?

The Parable
of the Builders

This parable from Matthew chapter seven and Luke chapter six lends itself to a visual demonstration. This skit requires only the narrator to learn any lines, with a few exceptions. Others mime out what is narrated, so this is a good skit to use if you have to pull something together quickly. This is not a very serious presentation of the parable, but it does get the point across.

Cast

Narrator—This character says all the lines so he should be a good storyteller with good timing.

Builder 1—A hard-working builder. The part only has two lines, but lots of movement.

Builder 2—A lazy builder. The part only has two lines but lots of movement.

House People—Six people whose bodies will make up the houses. You can use the same people for both houses, or different people. The chimney should be a tall person. House people need to be able to stand still in odd positions.

Flood People—A rowdy crowd of five or more who will mime a torrential flood. One of them speaks twice. They make a lot of loud noises.

Costumes

The narrator can wear casual clothes or dress up, depending on the play's setting. Builders can wear jeans. Girls who are house people should not wear skirts. They can wear matching colors if desired.

Flood people should wear blue. They could also carry and tie onto themselves blue scarves to suggest flowing water.

Production Notes

This scene will be most entertaining if the house people get into place really quickly. You can use volunteers selected just before the play to be house people if you wish to involve the audience, but it's a good idea to rehearse them for at least ten or fifteen minutes so they can respond quickly to cues. You may want to read the parable to the audience before the skit begins.

The Script

Narrator enters and remains in the sidelines throughout the play.

NARRATOR: One time Jesus said to a big crowd, "There's no point in saying you believe in me if you don't do what I say. Let me show you what a person's like when he hears my words and goes ahead and does them. That person is like someone . . .

(Narrator gestures as Builder 1 enters, miming carrying a shovel over his shoulder. He stops near C.)

. . . who decided to build his house on a solid rock. He dug his foundation way down deep into that rock . . .

(Builder 1 digs with great effort, pauses, panting, wipes his brow.)

. . . built his house from there, with four good walls . . .

(Four of the six house people run on as Builder 1 drops his shovel, then carefully places them at the four corners of his building, shifting them a few times to get it exactly right.)

. . . and a water-tight roof . . .

(House people face the person opposite them and put their arms up together in one sharp movement to make a roof.)

... with a straight, tall chimney ...

(One house person runs on and Builder 1 places him behind the other four, off-center, putting arms straight in the air and bending hands in flat to form the shape of a chimney which sticks up higher than the roof.)

... and an automatic garage door.

(The last house person runs on and Builder 1 places her to one side of the house, with hands at sides, facing the audience. Builder 1 steps forward to get the audience's attention and mimes pressing a remote-control garage door opener. The person begins to slowly raise her arms while making a mechanical sound effect, then halts with arms straight up. Builder 1 presses the remote again and the reverse takes place. Builder 1 looks pleased.)

BUILDER 1: Excellent.

NARRATOR: The builder was content because he knew he had a well-built house ...

(Builder 1 steps back, admires the house, then goes into it, miming opening and closing the front door and then looking out a front window.)

... Now it just so happened that some really bad storms came to that area, and caused flash floods. You know, the kind that wipes everything out before you know what hit you. Well, one of those floods came right to this house ...

(Flood people enter, swaying their arms back and forth, making roaring, gurgling, splashing noises. One of them yells above the noise.)

FLOOD PERSON: Mass destruction coming through!!

NARRATOR: ... It struck the brand new house ...

(Flood people rush at the house, making even louder noises, and swarm all over the house, not touching house people but getting very close, using wide, sweeping hand motions to suggest waves striking the house. Builder 1 is anxiously looking out the window, but house people stand firm. After fifteen or twenty seconds of attacking the house, flood people withdraw, decrease their noise level and run off the other side of the stage.)

FLOOD PERSON *(on the way out):* No fun man! This place is like, built on rock or something.

NARRATOR: . . . But the flood couldn't shake the house, because it was so well-built.

(Builder 1 comes out of the house, inspects it and stands back, smiling with relief.)

BUILDER: Way to be! *(Or a similar phrase.)*

(Narrator walks C to address the audience as everyone else quietly exits.)

NARRATOR: After he told the crowd about that builder. Jesus went on to talk about what people are like who don't do what He says. He said, "The one who hears my words and doesn't put them into practice is like a person . . .

(Narrator moves back to the sidelines and gestures as Builder 2 enters, miming carrying a shovel, and standing near C.)

. . . who built a house on sand, without a solid foundation . . .

(Builder 2 yawns, kicks around at the ground without much enthusiasm, starts to dig, can't make a hole in the sand, and gives up. He pitches his shovel and shrugs.)

. . . Now his house also had four walls . . .

(Four house people make a roof similar to the first one, but it's lopsided, and one person's arms are bent. Builder 2 tries to

straighten them but they fall back and he gives up and shrugs.)

. . . with a chimney . . .

(Another house person runs on and Builder 2 places him as the first chimney was, but this chimney leans noticeably to one side. Builder tries to straighten it, it leans again, and he gives up and shrugs.)

. . . and an automatic garage door. . . .

(Garage door person is placed as before, but this time when Builder 2 steps forward and hits his remote, the sound effect stutters, the arms go up in jerks and it stops halfway. Builder 2 presses the button a few more times, but nothing much happens. He gives up, pitches his remote upstage and shrugs. Builder 2 stands back and surveys the house.)

BUILDER 2: Well, it's no display home, but it'll make it—as long as some gigantic storm doesn't hit.

(Builder 2 goes into the house and looks out a window, as Builder 1 did. When he mimes opening the door, it sticks and he has to tug on it, then kicks it shut.)

NARRATOR: Well, it just so happened that another one of those floods came . . .

(Flood people enter, acting just as they did before.)

FLOOD PERSON: Mass destruction coming through!!

NARRATOR: . . . and struck the house.

(Flood rushes at the house as before, but this time it actually makes contact with house people, who all collapse to the floor right away, piling on top of Builder 2, who is screaming and ad–libbing about not having insurance. The flood people subside as before, this time laughing wickedly.)

FLOOD PERSON: Mission accomplished, Dudes. Well done!!

(After a moment of silence, the narrator continues.)

NARRATOR: It was completely destroyed.

(Builder 2 crawls out from under the collapsed house people, with difficulty, groans and surveys his destroyed house.)

BUILDER 2: Bummer. *(Or a similar expression.)*

(Narrator moves in to C to conclude as all others exit, Builder 2 shaking his head as he goes. After a pause, the narrator continues.)

NARRATOR: So, the point of the story is, even though it might seem harder to follow Jesus than to live your own way, the ones who stick with Jesus are the ones who'll still be standing in the end.

(Narrator exits.)

Questions for Discussion

1. What was the difference between the two builders in the parable?

2. How do you think this parable is like real life when it comes to doing what Jesus teaches?

3. What are some examples of how obeying Jesus' teaching gives you a solid life?

4. Can you think of a time when you did something that was wrong by God's standards because it seemed easier at the time than doing the right thing? What was the result?

The Parable of the Widow Who Wouldn't Give Up

This parable from Luke chapter eighteen urges people not to give up praying. The skit is short and uses three people.

Characters
Narrator—The narrator has most of the lines.

Judge—A mean person.

Widow—A poor, old lady.

Costumes
The narrator can wear casual clothes or dress up, depending on the setting for the skit. The widow should wear a long dress or skirt, a shawl on her head, and carry a shabby bag. She could also carry a cane. The judge can wear a black robe and maybe a curly white wig.

Production Notes
Before the scene starts, place a high-backed chair and table or desk at C for the judge. You could also use a pulpit with a stool behind it to give him more elevation. In the skit, the widow will mime knocking at and using a door. This is done so the audience can see her changing attitude as she approaches and knocks on the door. The person playing the widow should take care to mime in such a way that the door and its handle stay in the same place. Taping the floor makes it easier. You may want to read the parable to the audience before you perform the skit.

The Script

(Narrator enters R and stands to one side of the performing space.)

NARRATOR: One time, Jesus told his disciples a parable to show them that they should always pray and not give up. Here's how it went: In a certain town there was a mean judge who didn't believe in God and didn't care about people.

(Judge enters with a gavel, looking mean. He sits and pounds the gavel on his table.)

JUDGE *(to audience):* I'm a mean ol', tough ol', gruff ol' judge, You mess with me and I hold a grudge.

NARRATOR: Not a real popular guy. There was a widow in the same town who didn't have much money or power, and someone had ripped her off. She went to the judge and asked him to get justice done for her.

(Widow enters L, mimes knocking at a door and entering timidly.)

WIDOW *(quietly, with respect):* Sorry to bother Your Excellency, but I need you to bring down some justice for me.

NARRATOR: A reasonable request to make of a judge. But the judge said:

JUDGE *(waving her away):* I have more important things to do, than worry 'bout a little ol' widow like you.

(Widow looks disappointed, wrings her hands and leaves, remembering to open and shut the invisible door. As the narrator continues, the judge gets a paper and reads it; possibly one of those sensational weeklies.)

NARRATOR: So, the widow went away disappointed, but she couldn't let it rest, and pretty soon she decided to try again.

(Widow reenters, knocks more confidently and enters sooner. This time she speaks louder. She's nervous but determined.)

WIDOW: I don't mean to pester Your Excellency, but if you don't defend us, who else will it be?

NARRATOR: But the judge still didn't pay much attention.

JUDGE *(looking over his paper, cold and rude):* Just go and take yourself on home. Leave us superior folks alone!

(Widow looks displeased. She fixes her gaze on the judge for a few seconds and puts her hand on her hip.)

JUDGE *(rising out of his seat):* Go on now!

(Widow shakes her head and reluctantly exits. During the following narration, the judge sits and mutters, then gets up and paces back and forth.)

NARRATOR: So the widow left, but she knew she was being done wrong, and she couldn't let it go. She wasn't real excited about dealing with that judge again, but she got up her courage anyway, and marched back there.

(Widow reenters, looking determined, knocks confidently, takes a deep breath and enters.)

WIDOW: I must hold my ground here, Your Excellency, I will pound on this door till I get what I need!

NARRATOR: Well, this time the judge really blew up.

(The judge stomps over to the widow and glares down at her.)

JUDGE *(yelling):* Read my lips and hear me shout, You're not gonna change my mind—Get Out!

(Widow glares back at him, not flinching.)

NARRATOR: But the widow didn't back down.

WIDOW: You haven't seen the last of me—Your Excellency!

(She turns on her heel and marches out, slamming the imaginary door.)

NARRATOR: After the widow left, the judge got to thinking.

(Judge paces a few seconds, scratching his chin. Then he stops and talks to himself.)

JUDGE *(pacing and thinking between his lines):* That widow bothers me. She disturbs my peace. . . . If that woman keeps pounding on my door, getting more uppity with every visit, it's gonna make my life into a misery. . . . She'll wake me up from my naps. She'll embarrass me in front of my politically significant friends. She might even get me to feeling guilty, which would be the worst of all. . . . Well, I guess there's only one thing to do. Even though I don't believe in God or care about people, I'm gonna have to give her what she needs, because if I don't, she'll wear me out!

(He exits through the invisible door.)

NARRATOR: After Jesus told that story, he explained that God is nothing like that judge because He loves us so much. Jesus said that if a mean person who doesn't care about people can be convinced into giving justice, then how much more will God give His children what they need when they keep crying out to Him. So the point of the story is, keep praying and never give up on God.

Questions for Discussion

1. Why did the judge end up giving in to the widow?

2. How is God different than that judge?

3. Do you think we have to bother and pester God to get what we need? What kind of attitude does God's character deserve?

4. When you close your eyes and think about God, do you imagine that He is like a very loving father, or do you have other thoughts about Him? Take some time to discuss your feelings about God. *(Sometimes in our hearts we have a negative view of God even though our beliefs tell us He is good. If this is true, it helps to realize it and admit it, so we can ask God to help us understand, deep down, what He is really like.)*

5. Can you tell any stories about God answering your prayers? Did He always answer right away?

The Circle

This play explores how an addiction gradually develops, robs a person of choice and traps her in despair. Drug addiction might be the first thing people think of when they see the scene, but it can open discussion on other addictions such as addiction to a relationship or a certain activity. A circle on the stage floor represents the sphere of drug or other addiction experience.

Cast

Beth—An insecure girl who is lured into the circle. Her performing needs to convey the strange experiences she is going through. This character could be a male.

John—A persuasive, attractive person who entices Beth into the circle. He is cool and confident. This character could be female.

Paula—This is a smaller role than the other two. She is asleep most of the time and does not talk much until the end of the scene. Her manner is calm and apathetic, as though she were sedated. This character could be male.

Costumes

Beth wears ordinary casual clothes. John wears ordinary clothes or he can look tough. Paula looks like she has not made much effort with her appearance.

Production Notes

This is an easy play to set up—all you need is a long rope to define the circle *(at least a 10 foot diameter)* and 2 chairs or blocks together inside the circle, US, for Paula to lie on.

If you have any stage lighting, you can dim it during the times when there is a pause after John and Beth have both exited, to suggest the passage of time.

The Script

The play begins with Paula asleep on the boxes and John standing at the edge of the circle on the left side. John is looking offstage L. Beth enters L and stops outside the circle.

John: Hi.

Beth: Hi. So this is the circle, huh.

John: This is it. Are you gonna come in?

Beth: I don't know.

John: You want to, don't you?

Beth: I'm not sure.

John: Well you did come here, didn't you?

Beth: Yeah, I did do that.

John: You're gonna love it, Beth. It's a great place. I can't even describe it. You've just got to see it for yourself.

Beth *(peaking inside):* It does look pretty neat in there.

John: What are you waiting for?

Beth: Well, there's one thing that's bugging me. I've heard— some people are saying—that once you go in there, you can't get out.

John *(laughing):* That's not true. I come and go all the time. I come in, have a good time and go out again whenever I've got something else I have to do. Come on. Do you see anyone around here looking trapped?

Beth: Well, I can't see anyone from here. *(She looks inside; he positions himself so that her view of Paula is blocked.)*

John: All right.

Beth: But isn't it a magic circle? I mean, how do I know they didn't disappear or something? I've heard rumors.

John: OK—look. I have heard that some people have been known to, uh, abuse the place. And maybe they did kind of get stuck. But hey—just because a few suckers *(or a similar word)* don't know when to quit doesn't mean we should miss out on a good time.

BETH: Well how do you know what you should and shouldn't do in there?

JOHN: All right. How about this; how about I only take you where I've already been. You know I'm OK. *(He steps outside the circle to illustrate.)* So if you just go where I've been you'll be safe. How does that sound?

BETH: I guess that would be OK.

(He takes her hand and they step into the circle. Beth looks around for a few seconds.)

BETH: Hey, wait a minute. I don't know if I like it in here. It feels kind of funny. It makes me dizzy.

JOHN *(supports her, holding her shoulder):* That's all right. Everyone feels like that when they first come in. You'll get used to it.

BETH: Promise?

JOHN: Sure. Take another step. *(He leads her to the next clockwise step around the front of the circle, DSR.)*

BETH: Wait a minute! Everything looks really weird now. This is making me nervous.

JOHN: Hey, listen. Your problem is that you're all uptight. *(Starts to rub her neck.)* You're bringing in a bunch of junk from the outside. Forget everything. . . . Now how do you feel?

BETH: A little better.

JOHN: Look over there. *(Points out over the audience.)* How does that look now.

BETH: Uh, that looks kind of good. Yeah, that's nice.

JOHN *(pushing her just slightly, so that she moves another clockwise step):* What about from here?

BETH *(staring, mesmerized):* Hey, that's really nice. It looks so different. I mean, it's ordinary stuff, but it's so, awesome *(or a similar word).*

(By now she's looking stoned.)

JOHN *(smiles):* Keep going. That's nothing.

(She takes another step, looks around and laughs as though she is really enjoying a good joke.)

BETH: Hey, that's funny. *(She laughs for a moment, then settles down.)* Hey John, you were right. This place is all right.

JOHN: What'd I tell you.

BETH *(looking at her watch):* Oh—I've gotta be somewhere. Listen, could we do this again?

JOHN: Sure. I'm heading out too. I'll meet you back here.

BETH: OK, see you.

(They leave the circle and exit in opposite directions. Paula then wakes, sits up and looks around.)

PAULA: Anyone here?

(When there is no answer, she lies down and sleeps again. After a pause, John reenters and looks down at Paula. He shakes his head in a superior, judgmental way, then sees Beth reenter, and goes to welcome her.)

JOHN: Hey, you're back.

BETH *(happy and excited):* Yeah, I couldn't wait to get in again.

JOHN: I'll take you a little farther this time. *(He takes her hand and she steps into the circle.)* Come right over here. You're not gonna believe what it's like over here. *(He takes her directly through the circle and to the DR side, spinning her around. She stops, steadies herself and looks around. Her expression becomes dreamy.)*

JOHN: How do you like it?

(She smiles, sighs, and begins to lean sideways. John supports her and she leans heavily on him. She speaks with a slur.)

BETH: Mmmm. This is really nice. Everything's kind of—floating.

JOHN: You like that?

BETH: Yeah . . . There's nothing to worry about—everything just floats around and there's nothing to do but just—watch it float around. *(She looks around, head and eyes following the motions of floating objects.)* Look, bubbles too.

JOHN *(sightly amused):* Is that right?

BETH: Yeah! Hey John—you're floating too!

JOHN *(smiles):* Sure I am.

BETH *(looks at her hand):* My hand's floating too. There's nothing better than watching your hand float.

JOHN: That's what I always say.

BETH: Everything's floating away now. *(She calls out to whatever she is watching, which wakes Paula.)* Bye . . .

PAULA: Hey, what's going on?

JOHN: Oh, hi Paula. This is Beth. We were just watching stuff float. You know.

PAULA: Sounds like you were having a pretty good time.

BETH: Oh, I was. You wouldn't believe it. It was so peaceful, and it seemed it didn't matter what happened and everything I looked at was really . . .

PAULA *(nodding):* Yeah, I've been there.

BETH: Oh, right. *(Looks around.)* It's a little uh, ordinary when you come back, isn't it?

PAULA: A little. But you can always go back again.

JOHN: Right.

BETH *(calming down):* Yeah, you're right. *(Pauses, thinks.)*

87

Hey, what time is it? *(Looks at her watch.)* Uh-oh. I've been here for a long time. I wonder if I was supposed to be somewhere else? I don't really remember. Um, well—maybe I better go—I'm pretty sure I need to go.

PAULA: So are you coming back?

BETH: Hey, definitely. Soon as I can. Later.

(Gives John five and exits.)

PAULA *(to John):* Are you leaving too?

JOHN: Yup.

PAULA: Why don't you stick around a little longer?

JOHN *(unkindly):* I know when I've had enough.

(He exits. Paula looks after him wistfully, sighs, goes back to sleep. After a pause, Beth enters and steps quickly into the circle by herself. She's furious. She looks around, then wakes Paula.)

BETH: Paula—where's John?

PAULA: I don't know. I guess he'll be here soon.

(John reenters and steps into the circle. Paula sits up.)

PAULA: Here he is now.

BETH: Oh, there you are.

JOHN: You didn't waste any time getting back here.

BETH: That's for sure. I hate it out there. I hate school, I hate my job, I hate everything. I live with a bunch of jerks. I went home and I was already bummed out, because I was thinking of how boring it is out there, you know, compared to here, and I get home, and I was late for some dumb thing and they all jumped on my case like I was a criminal or something.

JOHN: Yeah, it's like that out there sometimes. People are pretty weird. But—hey—you've got an alternative, right?

BETH: Yeah, yeah, you're right.

JOHN: So you're here now. Forget about everything else. *(He reaches out his hand, she takes it and steps into the circle.)* You know, you need something to make you forget all this garbage. I think it's time you checked it out over here . . .

(He spins her around to the far side of the circle. She comes out of the spin, steadies herself and looks around in wonder. She is fascinated, animated. Paula is watching.)

BETH: Whoooo! What's going on! This is unreal. The ground's sort of crumbling underneath me, like it's dissolving—but I'm not going anywhere!

(She opens her eyes very wide, holds out her arms as though balancing in midair. Continues to look around. She is overwhelmed by her perceptions and seems a little out of control of the way she moves, i.e. her head sways, etc.)

BETH: This is bizarre. Now all the walls are falling apart. But that's OK. It's sort of like Kansas—you know? Everything's flat . . . but this is purple . . . I mean, it smells purple . . . *(She becomes a little disturbed.)* Hey John, are you still there. *(She doesn't see John standing next to her.)*

JOHN: I'm right with you.

BETH: And all this stuff's happening to you too?

JOHN: Sure.

BETH: You can see that lake with all the eyes looking up out of it?

JOHN: Something like that.

BETH: OK. I just wondered if this was normal.

JOHN: You're doing great.

BETH: I think I'm coming back now, John . . . I can feel the roof of my mouth again . . . *(She closes her eyes, then suddenly her eyes open wide, she grabs her head in pain and groans.)*

JOHN: What's the matter?

BETH: Oh, my head.

JOHN: Your head hurts?

BETH: It's awful.

JOHN: Really? That's weird. My head's never hurt when I've been over here.

BETH *(after a pause, still with a hand on her head)*: What? . . . I thought you said nothing would happen to me that didn't happen to you!

JOHN: Well, it hasn't—till now.

BETH *(panicked)*: Then why does my head feel like this?

JOHN: I don't know. I mean, you can't predict everything. It is a magic circle.

BETH: You lied to me! You said you knew what was going on!

JOHN: Hey! Don't blame me for your headache!

BETH: Well I don't need this. *(She glares at him, furious.)* I'm out of here. *(She moves to leave the circle but John's voice stops her.)*

JOHN: Hey wait a minute. . . . You think it's gonna be better for you out there? *(She looks doubtful, rubs her head.)* If you don't feel any good in here, how do you think its gonna be out there?

BETH: I don't know. I'm mixed up.

PAULA: I know how you feel. I had a headache over there once.

(They turn to her, unaware that she was awake.)

BETH: Really?

PAULA: Yeah. I know what you need. You need to take a few spins around the whole circle. Then you'll feel really great.

BETH: Yeah?

JOHN: Hey, yeah! I haven't done that for a long time. That's the best.

PAULA: Why don't you give it a try?

BETH: I feel so bad I'll try anything.

PAULA: You'll be OK. Go for it.

JOHN: Come here. *(He takes both her hands.)* All you've gotta do is hold on. Let's go!

(He stands in the center of the circle and holding both her hands, pivots her around at increasing speed. Beth reacts like someone on a roller-coaster ride, frightened but enjoying it at the same time. She starts saying things like "Oh Wow," and "This is wild," etc., but after five or six spins she starts to call out for him to stop.)

BETH *(laughing):* Hey, wait a minute. Stop. I'm so dizzy. Stop. *(He slows down and stops.)* Whew—I don't believe that! I didn't know there was anything like that!

JOHN: I know what you mean. What about your headache?

BETH *(thinks for a few seconds—she's forgotten she had one):* Oh, yeah. Yeah, it's gone. I forgot I even had one. Oh, hey, I'm sorry I got mad at you. I don't know why I got so paranoid.

JOHN: Oh, that's OK. Don't worry about it. *(He notices his watch.)* Ooh, listen, I just remembered I've got something I've gotta do on the outside now, so I'll meet you guys back here later, OK?

PAULA: Sure John.

BETH: Sure. *(Looks at her watch.)* Anyway, I really oughta be going now too. I've been in here an awful long time. I can't even keep track anymore.

JOHN: OK, see you next time. *(He steps out of the circle and exits.)*

BETH *(to Paula):* Well, this was pretty wild. Maybe I'll see you next time.

PAULA: Oh yeah, I'll be here.

(Beth goes to the circle entrance. She goes to walk out, but stops short of the edge; her hand has come up against an invisible barrier. She mimes feeling the barrier with both hands, surprised.)

BETH: Hey, what's going on.

PAULA: What.

BETH *(tries again to move forward):* I can't step forward. *(She steps back and tries again, but the same thing happens.)* This is stupid. It's like something is pushing me back from the edge. Like the wrong side of a magnet or something. *(She's getting scared. She tries standing sideways and pushing, reaches higher, reaches lower, etc., but nothing works.)* Paula—I can't get out!

PAULA: Take it easy.

BETH: What do you mean, take it easy—I can't get out of here! *(Calls.)* John, hey John, come back! I need you to get me out of here!

PAULA: He can't hear you.

BETH *(yells louder):* John—come back here. Help me! I can't get out! John!! *(Pauses, realizes it's futile.)* John? *(Another pause, she turns to Paula.)* Do you know what's going on?

PAULA *(quietly, sympathetically):* Yeah.

BETH: What?

PAULA: You can't get out.

BETH *(steps toward her):* What do you mean, I can't get out? How do you know I can't get out?

PAULA: I can't either.

BETH: You can't? *(Paula shakes her head.)* Not ever?

PAULA: I guess not. Every time I go to the edge something pushes me back.

BETH: But he said if I did what he did I'd be safe. He can get out! *(Paula shrugs.)* Well why didn't you tell me this could happen?

PAULA: I don't know. I guess I figured it was no big deal. I mean, it is better in here than out there.

BETH: No big deal? To be trapped? It's like being in jail!

PAULA: Hey, after a while you realize it's not so bad. Remember just a few minutes ago you thought this was the best place in the world? Well there's still everything in here you came for. If you feel bad, just go stand in one of those other places and let the magic take you somewhere.

BETH: I don't want to go to any magic place. I want to go home. *(She goes back to the edge and looks out.)*

PAULA *(rises and goes to Beth):* Listen. Why don't you come and sit down over here with me. It's a really nice place. It's a really peaceful place. Pretty soon you'll just go to sleep, and you'll have some great dreams, and when you wake up you won't care about it so much.

(Beth looks at Paula in despair, and allows Paula to lead her back to the blocks and be seated.)

PAULA: That's better. Don't worry now. You'll feel fine in a little while. *(She folds her arms and leans her head on her knees.)*

BETH: Paula?

PAULA: Hmm? *(Lifts her head slightly.)*

BETH: What's gonna happen to us?

PAULA *(sleepily):* I don't know. *(She closes her eyes and lowers her head.)*

(Beth looks around, looks down at Paula, then stands resolutely and walks to the entrance of the circle, pressing her hands against the invisible barrier.)

BETH: There's got to be some way out of here. There's got to be.

(She freezes.)

Questions for Discussion

This scene raises a lot of issues about addiction, and it would be best for the discussion leader to have some understanding of the area. If no one is available, make sure the discussion leader conveys the information included with the questions below, and doesn't present his opinions as facts.

1. What do you think the circle represented? *(Get answers besides alcohol and other drugs. Some other addictions include gambling, eating disorders like anorexia and bulimia, and sexual addictions such as pornography. This play provides a good opportunity for you to address the fact that lots of people are trapped in addictions, including Christians. An addiction is when a person is out of control of his behavior and he keeps repeating something even though it goes against his goals and values.)*

2. What did Beth like about the circle? *(excitement, new experiences, rebellion, good feelings, escape)* What price did she pay for the highs?

3. How did John persuade her to try it for the first time? *(Talk about peer pressure and the different forms it takes.)*

4. What do you think was happening to the rest of Beth's life when she wasn't in the circle?

5. Did all the characters get trapped? *(Use the fact that John didn't get trapped to point out that some people can get addicted faster than others, and you can't assume that because one person is abusing something without getting hooked, that you won't get hooked. This is especially true with alcohol and other drugs because our bodies respond to chemicals in different ways.)*

6. Do you think people like Beth and Paula can get out? How does someone get out of an addiction? *(Stress that there is always a way out, but that addicted people need out-*

side help. Rarely can you stop without treatment. Stress the need to talk to someone you trust so they can work with you on getting the help you need. Explain that chemical addictions need treatment in a hospital program first, then people need ongoing support to stay sober, from support groups such as Alcoholics Anonymous. With other kinds of habits that people are out of control with, a good first step is to get into counseling.)

(End this discussion by giving out the names of people in the church who are ready to talk to anyone who is concerned about his own or someone else's behavior. Make sure these people are ready with good referral sources, and that they are prepared to be nonjudgmental, confidential and give ongoing support.)

Three Ways
to Mess Up
a Relationship

This piece is made up of three skits which illustrate how peace and unity between people is destroyed by wrong behavior. Sometimes Christians give a lot of attention to the more sensational sins, such as breaking the law and sexual immorality, without recognizing that sins like gossip, slander and exclusiveness are forbidden by Scripture and are very damaging to relationships.

Discussion can follow each skit if you present all three together. They can also be performed apart as separate skits. If you do them altogether, you may want to give a brief introduction, explaining that you are doing the skits to take a closer look at how our behavior affects other people.

Characters

Skit One—In "Gossip" there are five people, Rhonda and four others.

Skit Two—In "Triangles" there are three girls. Angie is a troublemaker, Caroline is self-righteous and Diane is passive.

Skit Three—In "Cliques" there is one main character, the New Girl, and three small cliques of people, the Sports Clique (three members), the Music Clique (four members) and the Dating Clique (three females).

Costumes

People are dressed for church in all the skits.

Production Notes

The skits don't require any props and characters remain standing. All skits are conversations taking place in a church lobby, before a youth group meeting.

Skit One—Gossip

The scene begins with all five characters lined up across the stage with their backs to the audience. Rhonda is in the far right position. She turns to the front, looks at the person next to her, fidgets nervously, then taps Person 2 on the shoulder, who turns around too.

RHONDA: Hi.

PERSON 2: Hi Rhonda. How are you doing?

RHONDA: I need to talk to someone but this is really personal.

PERSON 2: What's the matter? You can tell me.

RHONDA: You wouldn't tell anyone?

PERSON 2: No way.

RHONDA: I'm so worried about my brother. He ran away last night.

PERSON 2: Oh no.

RHONDA: Yeah. He was having a fight with my dad and it was awful. They both got so mad . . . then this morning he was gone.

PERSON 2: That's terrible. Do you know where he went?

RHONDA: I don't know. That's what scares me. He was so angry, I'm afraid he'll do something really dumb like break the law and go somewhere so far away we can't find him.

PERSON 2: Well take it easy Rhonda. You don't have to think about stuff like that. He's probably just hiding out at a friend's place.

RHONDA: I guess you're right. Well, I better get into Sunday school. *(Or whatever you call it.)*

PERSON 2: Are you sure you're OK?

RHONDA: Yeah, thanks. I'll talk to you later.

PERSON 2: Keep me posted. Take it easy.

RHONDA: Yeah.

(She turns her back to the audience as Person 3 turns to the front and sees Person 2, who is still shaking her head.)

PERSON 3: What's going on?

PERSON 2: Oh, nothing.

PERSON 3: Well, why are you shaking your head?

PERSON 2: Oh man. *(Looking around carefully.)* Can you promise to keep a secret? I just heard something and I can't believe it.

PERSON 3: What?

PERSON 2: Promise?

PERSON 3: OK, promise. What?

PERSON 2: Rhonda's brother ran away from home last night.

PERSON 3: Really?

PERSON 2: Yeah. She's really worried about him.

PERSON 3: Do they know where he went?

PERSON 2: No. Sounds like her old man said something really bad or hit him or something and he couldn't handle it so he ran. She's all worried he'll do something dumb like steal a car and go to Florida or something. I tried to calm her down.

PERSON 3: That's really serious.

PERSON 2: Yeah, could be. Just keep a lid on it, OK?

PERSON 3: Sure.

(Person 2 turns her back to the audience. Person 3 thinks the news over for a minute. He looks over at Person 4's turned

back a few times, thinks again, then finally taps Person 4 on the shoulder, he turns around.)

PERSON 4: Oh hi. How are you?

PERSON 3: Well I'm OK, but Rhonda's not doing too well.

PERSON 4: How come?

PERSON 3: Well, I'm not supposed to say anything. I'm only telling you so you can pray about it.

PERSON 4: OK.

PERSON 3: Her big brother took off last night.

PERSON 4: Seriously?

PERSON 3: Yeah. It's bizarre. They seemed like a pretty cool family, but it sounds like the dad's been beating him up, so he took off. They think he stole a car. He could be in Florida by now for all they know.

PERSON 4: That's wild. It's hard to believe.

PERSON 3: I know, but it's true. You never can be sure what's really going on with people. Hey, don't say anything to Rhonda, OK? I'm not supposed to know.

PERSON 4: Uh-huh.

(Person 3 turns back away from the audience, Person 4 looks at Person 5. He thinks for a while about whether to spread the news, but not as long as Person 3 did. He taps Person 5, who turns around.)

PERSON 5: Hi.

PERSON 4: Hi, you're not gonna believe what I just heard. It blew me away.

PERSON 5: What?

PERSON 4: Well, most people don't know about it yet, but Rhonda's brother ran away.

PERSON 5: Oh, no.

PERSON 4: The dad's been beating him up so much he just couldn't put up with it anymore.

PERSON 5: What? You're kidding.

PERSON 4: That's what I heard.

PERSON 5: I know her family. I never would have guessed that in a million years.

PERSON 4: I know. But that's not all. He stole a car and they caught up with him all the way down in Florida. I wonder what'll happen to him.

PERSON 5: Rhonda must be so upset.

PERSON 4: I know. I can't believe she came to church.

PERSON 5: She's here?

PERSON 4: Yeah, I saw her come in earlier.

PERSON 5: I'm glad you told me.

PERSON 4: Well, you're trustworthy.

PERSON 5: Sure.

(Person 4 turns away from the audience. Person 5 looks around. She sees Rhonda on the other side of the stage, calls her and moves toward her as Rhonda turns around.)

PERSON 5: Hey, Rhonda!

RHONDA: Yeah?

PERSON 5: Hi.

RHONDA: Hi.

PERSON 5: I, uh, heard what happened. I'm really sorry.

RHONDA: What?

PERSON 5: Well, I don't really know what to say. I just wanted to say I'm sorry it happened. You must be so upset.

RHONDA: You know?

PERSON 5: Yeah.

RHONDA: About my brother?

PERSON 5: Well yeah, and I know how you feel. My cousin stole a car a few months ago and it was really hard for the whole family. When he went to court . . .

RHONDA *(shocked, angry):* What! Someone told you that?

PERSON 5: Well, yeah.

RHONDA: That didn't even happen. All we know is he ran away!

PERSON 5: Oh . . . wow, I'm sorry. I heard that he . . .

RHONDA: Who would have made up a thing like that?

PERSON 5: I don't know Rhonda. You know how stuff gets twisted around.

RHONDA: I don't believe this. I just don't believe this. I tell one person he ran away and now everybody thinks he's a criminal!

(She looks around with a shocked expression, then runs off R. All the others see her, and turn sideways, watching her exit.)

PERSON 5 *(to person 4):* I didn't know it was a secret. She was ticked.

PERSON 4: Oh no, you didn't say anything to her did you?

PERSON 5: Well, I didn't know! I just wanted to make her feel better!

PERSON 3 *(to Person 4)*: Wait a minute. You mean you told her when you promised to keep it a secret? Oh great. Way to go!

PERSON 2 *(to Person 3):* What's the deal? I thought you said you could keep a secret!

PERSON 3 *(louder):* Look who's talking! You're the one who started this!

(They all exit L, continuing to argue and blame each other as they go.)

Skit Two—Triangles

Diane is standing near C. Angie storms on R, in a huff, sees Diane and joins her.

ANGIE: Diane, I am so mad I'm going to explode.

DIANE: What happened?

ANGIE: It's Caroline. I am so sick of her thinking she's Queen of the Universe or something. I was just telling her how I got into trouble at the lock in last night and she said she thinks I deserved it!

DIANE: She said that?

ANGIE: Well, sort of. I mean, I was telling her because I thought it was funny. I mean it was—wasn't it?

DIANE: Well yeah. Most people don't have the guts to cover the senior minister's car with cream-filled cookies.

ANGIE: I thought she would laugh, but she started telling me how irresponsible I was. She went into this big lecture about how I could have gotten hurt climbing out of the church window and then the church could have gotten into legal trouble and that it wasn't right to do that to the minister, and on and on. Give me a break.

DIANE: She is kind of hyper-mature.

ANGIE: She's hyper-obnoxious. I swear, I . . .

DIANE *(looking offstage R):* Shh. Here she comes.

(Caroline enters R and joins the other two.)

CAROLINE: Hi.

DIANE & ANGIE: Hi.

(Angie has her arms crossed and looks ticked-off.)

CAROLINE: So, what's going on?

DIANE *(a little awkward):* Uh, not much.

CAROLINE: You guys want to get some ice cream after the meeting?

(Diane looks at Angie, who makes no response.)

DIANE: Uh, yeah, OK.

CAROLINE: What about you Angie?

ANGIE *(shrugging):* I don't know. I'm gonna go get a seat.

(She exits L. Caroline watches her until she is gone.)

CAROLINE: I don't know what her problem is lately. She's always bent out of shape about something and I never know what.

DIANE: Really?

CAROLINE: I mean constantly. Ever since she broke up with her boyfriend she's been acting like the whole world hates her. Isn't it driving you crazy?

DIANE: I guess she does get pretty angry sometimes.

CAROLINE: Sometimes? You mean all the time.

DIANE: Well, yeah.

CAROLINE: She treats everyone like scum. Don't you get tired of it? I mean, she does it to you too.

DIANE: She is kind of grotty *(or a similar word)* these days.

CAROLINE: I think she should get a grip. I'm not going to put up with it much . . .

DIANE *(looking offstage L):* Shh. She's coming back.

(Angie reenters and approaches them. Diane looks around for an excuse to escape the tension.)

ANGIE: Are you two coming or what?

DIANE: Oh, I think Steve's saving a seat for me.

(She exits L. The other two are tense about being alone. They

look at each other, then look away. They start to talk at the same time, then laugh nervously.)

CAROLINE: I was just going to ask if you were going to Jannine's party next weekend.

ANGIE: Oh, yeah. I'm probably gonna go.

CAROLINE: Well, if you need a ride I can get my dad to pick you up. *(Or, if she's over 16, "I can pick you up.")*

ANGIE *(softening at the friendly overture):* That would be good.

CAROLINE: OK. It's at eight.

ANGIE: Are you gonna get Diane first?

CAROLINE *(glancing around to make sure Diane is gone):* Uh, well, I think I'll let Diane get her own ride. She's so late all the time, I'm afraid she'd hold us up.

ANGIE: Oh, OK.

CAROLINE: She's kept me waiting a lot.

ANGIE: Yeah, I know what you mean.

CAROLINE: Don't tell her I said that. She'd die if she knew we were talking about her.

ANGIE: Oh I know. I won't.

(They exit L.)

Skit Three—Cliques

New Girl enters R, stands C and addresses audience.

NEW GIRL: Well, here I am at our new church. I wish I hadn't moved. I don't know anyone in my neighborhood. I don't know anyone in my school. I don't know anyone at this church. I hope they're nice here. Everyone at school was so cliquey.

(Sports clique enters; Sports 1 from the R and Sports 2 and 3 from L. Sports 1 crosses in front of New Girl to meet them.)

SPORTS 2: Hey, where were you last night? It was the most awesome game of the century!

SPORTS 1: Tell me about it. You were watching it on TV; I was there.

SPORTS 3 *(to Sports 2):* He's lying.

SPORTS 1: I do not tell a lie. Blue seats. Third row. Right on the first base line. There is no more to life.

SPORTS 2: You scum-bucket! *(Or a similar term.)* I'd love to be at the play-offs. How'd you get a ticket?

SPORTS 1: One of my dad's buddies had to fly out of town. Someone in his family was sick or dying or something. I got his seat.

SPORTS 2: Now that's a dude with some weird priorities.

(New girl has walked nearer to the group, and now timidly interrupts.)

NEW GIRL: Hi.

(They notice her for the first time, say quick hellos and proceed with their conversation.)

SPORTS 3: Yeah, that was a wild game. What a finish. _____ *(Name a left fielder.)* throws it to home plate and ends the game. Everyone was losing it.

SPORTS 2: It was sweet. I wish that's what life was like.

SPORTS 1: Really.

(New Girl tries again to break in.)

NEW GIRL: Uh, I've never been here before and I was wondering if you know where I should go for the high school meeting?

SPORTS 3: Yeah, that's where we're going. You go down that hall, *(Points L.)* then turn right, then you go left around two more corners then it's up these stairs and through a double door and then it's the third door on your right. I think.

NEW GIRL *(bewildered): Thanks.*

SPORTS 3: Sure.

(They resume their conversation again, ignoring her.)

SPORTS 1: Anyway, are you guys gonna keep playing volleyball with the church now that school's started?

SPORTS 2: I don't know. My mom says if my grades don't get better this year she's gonna ground me off all sports. She says I'm so into sports my brain's gonna end up like a soccer ball, nothing in it but air.

(They begin to exit L, leaving the New Girl alone. As they leave, they keep talking.)

SPORTS 3: Well don't get grounded. We need you for the football team or they'll make Dryer quarterback. Then we're at the bottom of the barrel for sure . . .

(As they exit, New Girl comes back DC to address the audience.)

NEW GIRL: Well, either I memorize fifty issues of "Sports Illustrated" or I live without them. Tough decision. Not.

(Music clique enters R and stands in a semicircle, talking animatedly together.)

NEW GIRL: Well, if at first you don't succeed . . .

(She approaches the clique, but none of them notice her.)

MUSIC 1: Well if you guys want me to get tickets for you too, I need the money up front tomorrow.

MUSIC 3: That's cool. I'll bring it to school.

MUSIC 4: How much?

MUSIC 2: $_____ *(Name the amount that big rock concerts cost in the city nearest you.)*

Music 4: Wow! That equals working at Whippy Dip for 10 hours. They'd better be hot.

Music 3: _____ *(Name a really popular group.)* are always hot.

New Girl *(stepping forward):* Hi you guys.

(They notice her for the first time, give brief greetings and continue talking.)

Music 2 *(to 3 & 4):* Why don't you guys come with us. Then we can trade off sleeping in the car.

Music 1: Yeah. I was out there all night last time with no break —in January. Froze my toes off. But I got third row seats.

(New Girl has been having trouble following the conversation. Finally she speaks up.)

New Girl: Uh, what are you guys going to?

(They look at her as though she has asked a very dumb question.)

Music 2: We're gonna stand in line tomorrow night to get good seats for the concert.

New Girl: What concert?

(They all look at one another and smirk.)

Music 1: _____ *(the group).* Who else.

Music 3: Have you been living in a cave lately?

New Girl: Sorry I asked.

(New Girl, offended, leaves the group and moves back DC to address the audience. Music clique exits L, talking as they go.)

New Girl *(to audience):* I think the kids at school are nicer. What I'm wondering is why people who would stand out on a city street all night in January would think I'm ignorant.

(Dating clique enters R and stands upstage off center, talking animatedly among themselves. New Girl looks back at them doubtfully.)

NEW GIRL *(to audience):* Well, what I'd really like to do about now is crawl into a hole, but I guess I should give it one more try. Third time lucky, maybe?

(She approaches the dating clique.)

DATING 1: I couldn't believe it when I saw those two together. I mean they have, like, nothing in common.

DATING 2: Well, people used to say that about me and DJ but we've been together three months now.

DATING 3: That's serious business, Girl.

DATING 2: Tell me about it.

DATING 1: Well, Jeff and I have tons of stuff in common.

DATING 3: Like what?

DATING 1: Well, we both like those new _____ from _____ *(name some new menu item from a fast-food chain),* and we both like red sports cars best of all, and the other day we were having this really heavy discussion and he said he was totally against child abuse, which is exactly how I feel.

NEW GIRL *(stepping forward):* Hi.

(Dating clique all greet her. They are friendlier than the other groups.)

DATING 2: Are you new here? I've never seen you before.

NEW GIRL: Yes, I just moved here. My name's Margaret.

DATING 3: Oh, nice to meet you. Well, I'm Stephanie. I'm dating Eric over there. *(She points.)*

DATING 2: I'm Alisha. I'm dating DJ, over there. *(She points.)*

DATING 1: I'm Dawn. I'm dating Jeff, over there. *(She points.)*

NEW GIRL: Oh.

DATING 1, 2, 3, *(all together to New Girl):* Are you dating anyone?

NEW GIRL *(taken aback):* Uh, no. I'm not.

(Hearing this, they lose interest in her.)

DATING 1, 2, 3: Oh.

(They immediately turn away and begin to exit L, leaving New Girl behind. They talk as they go.)

DATING 1: Jeff and I are going to a movie tonight.

DATING 3: I'm going to a party with DJ.

DATING 2: Eric and I decided to stay home and veg out.

(As they exit, New Girl returns DC to address audience. She is exasperated.)

NEW GIRL: I give up. If my parents make me come to this church again I'm going to run away to an airport and join up with the Moonies. At least they show a little interest.

(She exits R.)

Questions for Discussion

Skit One—Gossip

1. How did the facts change as the information about Rhonda's family was passed along?

2. Have you ever had a confidence broken? How did it feel?

3. Have you ever broken a confidence? How did you feel after you did it?

4. Why do you think people gossip?

5. What can you do when someone starts to tell you something and you know it's none of your business?

(You may want to discuss when it is not appropriate to keep a confidence; i.e. , when you find out someone is doing or plans to do something that could be harmful. Some examples of when not to keep a secret are when a friend says he's thinking about suicide, or when you hear that someone is being abused.)

Skit Two—Triangles

1. What did you notice about how the characters related to each other?

2. When it is used to describe relationships, the word "triangle" refers to people talking to someone else about a problem they are having with a person, instead of dealing directly with the person. The person being talked about is known by both. What are some examples of triangling in the skit?

3. Why do people triangle instead of talking directly to each other? *(Some reasons to discuss: it is less stressful than*

confronting someone head-on, it relieves tension, it makes us feel close to the person we are talking to.)

4. What effects do triangles have on relationships? *(Some effects: your relationship with the person you are having a problem with is damaged by your dishonesty, you don't get the problem solved, you put the third person in the awkward position of being stuck in the middle and knowing things they aren't supposed to know. That third person might decide that you are not to be trusted.)*

5. What should each of the girls have said directly to each other to keep their friendships honest? *(Try role-playing these direct conversations, instructing actors to get to the point but be loving and tactful. It's good practice for real life.)*

Skit Three—Cliques

1. How do you feel when you are at a new church or a new school?

2. Can you think of a time when you were left out of a group? How did it feel?

3. What are some of the unspoken rules that decide whether someone will be in or out of a group?

4. How do you think your church youth group does in the area of being friendly and accepting?

5. Why do people get into cliques that shut others out? How can a group of close friends avoid being seen as a "clique"?

6. What Bible verses can you think of that speak to this whole area of how we treat people? Does the Bible leave any room for the exclusive behavior you saw in the skit?